Letts

KS3

SUCCESS

ENGLISH

Author
Kath Jordan

CONTENTS

READING FICTION

READING POETRY

READING NON-FICTION

READING MEDIA TEXTS

WRITING

SHAKESPEARE

SPELLING, PUNCTUATION AND GRAMMAR

WHAT TO EXPECT IN YOUR EXAMS

At the end of Year 9 you will receive two National Curriculum levels. The first is from your **key stage 3 SATS** (Standard Assessment Tests), the second is your **Teacher Assessment level** given by your class teacher. This book is designed to help you achieve the best level you can.

ATTAINMENT TARGETS

The National Curriculum for English is split into three Attainment Targets.

- AT1 Speaking and Listening: this is not tested in your SATS but it does count towards your Teacher Assessment level.
- AT2 Reading: Both SATS papers test your understanding and response to a variety of written texts.
- AT3 Writing: Both SATS papers test your written expression and accuracy.

NATIONAL CURRICULUM LEVELS
Each Attainment Target is split into eight levels. The expected level for 14-year-olds is level 5. Your SATS exam result will be reported as a level for AT2, a level for AT3 and an *overall level*. Your Teacher Assessment level will be an overall level for AT1, AT2 and AT3. Each section of this book explains what you need to do to reach level 5 and above.

Exam Advice Check-list
- Look closely at the amount of time and the number of marks available for each question.
- Make sure you allow yourself time to check your answers carefully.
- Make sure you read the questions carefully and answer them fully.
- Follow the instructions.
- Plan your answers, especially in Paper 1C and Paper 2.
- Bring a watch into the exam or make sure you can see a clock.

READING PAPER

Time: 1 hour **plus** 15 minutes reading time

Assessment: **Reading** – understanding and response

Tasks: You will be given a reading booklet containing three texts or extracts. The texts included will be a combination of **fiction, non-fiction, media and poetry**. In a separate booklet, you will be required to answer about 15 questions. The style of the questions will be varied but may include:
- ticking a box or writing a one word answer
- finding and copying a quotation and explaining why it is effective
- writing an extended answer, focusing on language and structure

WRITING PAPER

Time: 1 hour and 15 minutes **including** planning time

Assessment: **Writing to:** imagine, explore, entertain **or**
inform, explain, describe **or**
persuade, argue, advise **or**
analyse, review, comment

Tasks: You will be required to complete **two** tasks that test your skills in two of the writing triplets listed above.

Task one is 45 minutes long and tests:
- sentence structure and punctuation
- text structure and organisation
- composition and effect.

Task two is 30 minutes long and tests:
- sentence and text organisation
- composition and effect
- spelling.

SHAKESPEARE PAPER

Time: 45 minutes

Assessment: **Reading** – understanding and response to **Shakespeare**

Tasks: You will be given a reading booklet containing two extracts from the Shakespeare play you have studied.
There will be **one** question. You will be required to write about **both** of the extracts from the play you have studied.

HOW TO IMPROVE YOUR SPEAKING AND LISTENING

Talking, discussing and sharing ideas are very useful ways to improve your understanding in other areas of English. Here are some ideas for improving your performance in some of the areas listed below.

ASKING QUESTIONS

This is an excellent way to improve your levels of understanding. Asking a question does not always mean that you don't understand what your teacher is talking about. If you do understand everything continue to ask questions. It allows you to look beneath the surface for less obvious meaning. You will be given credit for asking intelligent and searching questions.

ANSWERING QUESTIONS

You should always attempt to answer questions in group discussions or oral tests. Even if you get the answer wrong, you will be given credit for thinking and trying your best. If you don't feel sure of an answer you should still have a go. You may have approached the problem from another angle or thought of something that your teacher did not consider. It does happen!

INFORMAL DISCUSSION

You will often be asked to discuss work in small groups (not just in English). It might be a poem, a character's strengths and weaknesses, a new approach to a problem or a social issue. The key to success is to speak and listen. This will allow you to share information and develop new ideas before sharing them with a larger group. You will lose marks if you remain silent and just listen. You will also lose marks if you are aggressive or you talk too much and ignore the ideas of others.

ROLE PLAY

Take time to think about the main concerns and emotions of the character you are taking on. Think about the style of language your character would use: formal or informal, local slang or dialect, etc.

FORMAL DEBATE

There are rules and procedures to follow in a debate – your teacher will explain these to you. The important thing to remember is that you must use Standard English. Do not use slang, colloquialisms or dialect words. A debate is about listening to others as well as putting your own point across. You will develop a much stronger argument if you listen and respond to the points made by the opposition. Make sure that you listen to their points and respond to them as well as putting forward your arguments.

READING ALOUD

This is a skill that can only be developed with practice. Always speak clearly and stand or sit up straight. Read to the punctuation to maintain the sense of what you are reading. Think about the content of the piece you are reading. Try to express the emotions of the characters you are reading by varying the pace and tone of your voice.

Examiner's Top Tip
If you are not confident in Speaking and Listening then try to note down at least one point or question and make sure you use it in the debate or discussion.

TO ACHIEVE LEVEL 5 YOU NEED TO

- attempt to use <u>Standard English</u> in formal situations
- develop ideas and sequence events through talk
- ask <u>questions</u> to develop ideas
- <u>listen</u> carefully to the opinions and ideas of others

Examiner's Top Tip
L7: If you are confident about speaking in a group, then help others by asking supportive questions to bring in a weaker member of your group or by reinforcing a point made by somebody else.

TO MOVE FROM LEVEL 5 TO LEVELS 6 AND 7 YOU ALSO NEED TO

- make fluent and confident use of <u>Standard English</u> in formal situations
- <u>extend</u> your vocabulary
- <u>listen</u> and <u>respond</u> with sensitivity to the ideas of others
- engage the <u>interest</u> of your listener by varying <u>pace</u>, <u>tone</u> and <u>style</u> of presentation
- show an <u>awareness</u> of your audience by using appropriate <u>language</u>, <u>tone</u> and <u>pace</u>

SPEAKING & LISTENING

YOUR FINAL LEVEL FOR <u>SPEAKING AND LISTENING</u> IS DECIDED ON BY YOUR ENGLISH TEACHER. IT IS BASED ON YOUR PERFORMANCE OVER THE WHOLE OF YEAR 9.

TASKS YOU MIGHT EXPECT

- **answering questions in class**
- **asking questions in class**
- **informal paired discussion**
- **informal group discussion**
- **formal debate**
- **formal paired interviews on a specified topic**
- **giving a talk (formal or informal)**
- **reading aloud**
- **role play or drama.**

Have a go ...
1. Plan a talk on a subject you are interested in. Make a tape recording of your talk so you can work out how to improve your performance.
2. Choose a passage from your reading book and practise reading aloud at home.
3. Discuss your homework, the news or recent events in your favourite soap opera with a friend or your family.

IMAGERY

<u>Image</u>: a picture painted with words. You may pick out a sensory image or an image of war, etc.

<u>Metaphor</u>: an assertion that one object is a completely different object – there is no comparison made. Similar effect to <u>simile</u> but much more powerful. E.g. <u>His</u> <u>final</u> <u>words</u> <u>were</u> <u>icy</u> <u>splinters</u> <u>that</u> <u>lodged</u> <u>in</u> <u>her</u> <u>heart</u>.

- <u>Extended</u> <u>metaphor</u>: a <u>metaphor</u> built up in a longer section of writing. The extended metaphor could be built using <u>similes</u> and other <u>images</u>.

<u>Oxymoron</u>: the joining of two words or phrases that appear to be complete opposites in meaning. E.g. <u>Feather</u> <u>of</u> <u>lead</u>, <u>bright</u> <u>smoke</u>, <u>cold</u> <u>fire</u>, <u>sick</u> <u>health</u>, <u>Still</u> <u>waking</u> <u>sleep</u>. (*Romeo and Juliet* Act 1, Scene 1). This emphasises Romeo's dissatisfaction and confusion. He loves Juliet, a Capulet; he should hate her.

<u>Personification</u>: an inanimate object is given human qualities or attributes. E.g. <u>Well-apparell'd</u> <u>April</u> <u>on</u> <u>the</u> <u>heel/Of</u> <u>limping</u> <u>winter</u> <u>treads</u> (*Romeo and Juliet* Act 1 Scene 2). This compares the seasons of spring and winter to a young lover and an old man near the end of his life.

<u>Simile</u>: a comparison of two distinctly different objects using the words <u>like</u> or <u>as</u>. Used to make particular associations in the mind of the reader. E.g. <u>Some</u> <u>sat/poised</u> <u>like</u> <u>mud</u> <u>grenades</u> (a description of frogs).

Examiner's Top Tip
Try to use the correct technical terms when you are writing about literature.

STRUCTURE

<u>Caesura</u>: a pause in the middle of line of poetry or a sentence in prose, for dramatic effect. E.g. <u>Angry</u> <u>frogs</u> <u>invaded</u> <u>the</u> <u>flax-dam;</u> <u>I</u> <u>ducked</u> <u>through</u> <u>the</u> <u>hedges.</u>

<u>End-stopped</u> <u>line</u>: in poetry, a full stop or colon at the end of a line that causes the reader to pause. This is sometimes used for dramatic effect, particularly when used with <u>enjambment</u>.

<u>Enjambment</u>: run-on lines – when the meaning of a line 'runs on' to the next line without any mark of punctuation. Often used to show movement or excitement in a poem.

<u>Free</u> <u>verse</u>: describes a poem that has a free structure, without a regular <u>rhythm</u>, <u>rhyme</u> <u>scheme</u> or <u>stanza</u> length.

<u>Rhyme</u>: the ending of one word sounds the same as another e.g. <u>late/fate</u>; <u>sight/might</u>; <u>health/wealth</u>.

- **End rhymes** are most common. These are rhymes which occur at the end of a verse line.
- **Internal rhymes** occur in the middle of a line.
- **Rhyme schemes** are patterns of rhyme within a poem. Used for a variety of effects: to give structure; in comic verse; to link ideas.

<u>Rhythm</u>: the pattern of beats or stresses in a line or group of lines.

<u>Stanza</u>: a verse – a group of lines in poetry.

Examiner's Top Tip
Don't just <u>identify</u> images or devices. You must <u>explain</u> why they are effective.

DEVICE

<u>Alliteration</u>: the repetition of a letter or letter sound at the beginning of a sequence of words. Used for emphasis and to link ideas. E.g. **The silver snake slithered silently by**.

<u>Assonance</u>: the repetition of identical or similar vowel sounds in a sequence of words. E.g. **Silent, quiet, light, time** (long 'i' sound).

<u>Onomatopoeia</u>: the sound of a word reflects the sound that it describes. E.g. **plop, hiss, fizz, splash**.

A GLOSSARY OF LITERARY TERMS

USE THIS <u>GLOSSARY</u> AS YOU WORK THROUGH THE FOLLOWING CHAPTERS IN THIS BOOK.

OTHER TERMS

<u>Empathy</u>: writers put themselves in the place of the person or object they are writing about; a stronger sensation than sympathy. If you empathise with someone you can understand how they feel and feel their pain, sadness, relief, etc. yourself.

<u>Narrative</u>: a story, whether told in prose or poetic form.

- First-person narrative: events are narrated by a person involved in the story. E.g <u>I walked along the hard, stony ground</u>.
- Third-person narrative: events are narrated by an outside observer of the story. E.g. <u>He walked along the hard, stony ground</u>.

<u>Narrator</u>: the <u>storyteller</u>. Again you could have <u>first-</u> or <u>third-person narrators</u>.

PLOT

A well-constructed story-line will keep readers interested as they are keen to know how a story will develop. Many novels have sub-plots: minor story-lines that develop with the main plot. In a short extract it is only possible to work out what is happening at the time – you cannot comment on plot development.

Examiner's Top Tip
Although all of these elements are essential to fiction, authors will often give more weight to one feature than to others.

CHARACTERISATION

Writers try to know their characters very well – this helps to make them believable to the reader. We need to know what a character looks like; how they speak and behave; how they think and feel; how they get on with other characters. To maintain the flow of the plot it is not possible for a writer to directly tell us all of this information and so it is important to <u>read beneath the surface</u> for character development.

READING FICTION

Fiction is stories describing imaginary events and people.
Key ingredients in good fiction are:
- plot
- characterisation
- relationships
- setting
- use of language

This section will help you to identify these elements and make a <u>personal response</u> to fiction texts.

Examiner's Top Tip
Remember to identify <u>and</u> explain the effective use of these elements.

RELATIONSHIPS

We all have relationships – with family, friends, teachers or work colleagues. To be believable, fictional characters must develop relationships within a text. The development of a relationship can often be the central element of the plot.

SETTING

The setting of a piece of fiction, both in time and place, is very important. Setting can often be central to creating a particular atmosphere or reflecting the mood of a character.

USE OF LANGUAGE

Interesting use of language is what makes us keep on reading. To comment on the use of language in fiction you need to recognise the use of particular <u>devices</u> <u>and</u> <u>structures</u>, and the extent of the <u>detail</u> <u>and</u> <u>description</u>. Effective use of language will ensure that all of the other elements are brought to life. When thinking about language in fiction you should consider:

- choice of vocabulary
- adjectives
- adverbs
- sentence structure
- imagery – simile, metaphor, personification, etc.

Basic Questions

To help organise your thoughts, ask yourself four basic questions:

1. <u>What</u> is the story-line?
2. <u>Who</u> are the main characters?
3. <u>What</u> is their relationship?
4. <u>Where</u> is it set?

UNDERSTANDING FICTION

To achieve level 5 you need to:
- recognise what the <u>characters</u> are like
- have a general understanding of the whole text
- begin to read beneath the surface for <u>meaning</u>
- note the effect of particular <u>words</u> and <u>phrases</u>

To move from level 5 to levels 6 and 7 you also need to:
- comment on the writer's <u>use</u> <u>of</u> <u>language</u>
- comment on the <u>structure</u> of the text
- comment on the <u>creation</u> <u>of</u> <u>setting</u> <u>and</u> <u>atmosphere</u>
- recognise what the writer is <u>trying</u> <u>to</u> <u>achieve</u> and how they do this
- trace the <u>development</u> <u>of</u> <u>plot</u>, <u>character</u> <u>and</u> <u>relationships</u>
- give a <u>personal</u> <u>response</u> to the text.

EXAMPLE TEXT

I'M THE KING OF THE CASTLE BY SUSAN HILL

In this extract the boy, Kingshaw, has gone for a walk in the fields and has a very frightening experience.

Look for the ingredients:

- plot
- characterisation
- relationships
- setting
- use of language

See pages 13–14 where the text is explained.

THE TEXT

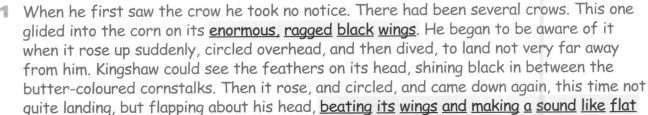

Extract from *I'm the King of the Castle* by Susan Hill

1   When he first saw the crow he took no notice. There had been several crows. This one glided into the corn on its <u>enormous, ragged</u> <u>black</u> <u>wings</u>. He began to be aware of it when it rose up suddenly, circled overhead, and then dived, to land not very far away from him. Kingshaw could see the feathers on its head, shining black in between the butter-coloured cornstalks. Then it rose, and circled, and came down again, this time not quite landing, but flapping about his head, <u>beating its wings and making a sound like flat</u> <u>leather pieces being slapped together. It was the largest crow</u> he had ever seen. As it came down for the third time, he looked up and noticed its beak, opening in a screech. <u>The inside of its mouth was scarlet</u>, it had small glinting eyes.

2   Kingshaw got up and flapped his arms. For a moment, the bird retreated a little way off, and higher up in the sky. He began to walk rather quickly back, through the path in the corn, looking ahead of him. <u>Stupid to be scared of a rotten bird. What</u> <u>could a bird do?</u> But he felt his own extreme isolation, high up in the cornfield.

3   For a moment, he could only hear the soft thudding of his own footsteps, and the silky sound of the corn, brushing against him. Then there was a rush of air, as <u>the</u> <u>great crow</u> came beating down, and wheeled about his head. The beak opened and the hoarse caw came out again and again, from inside the <u>scarlet mouth</u>.

4   Kingshaw began to run, not caring, now, if he trampled the corn, wanting to get away, down into the next field. He thought that the corn might be some kind of crow's food store, in which he was seen as an invader. <u>Perhaps this was only the</u> <u>first of a whole battalion of crows, that would rise up and swoop at him.</u> Get on the grass then, he thought, get on to the grass, that'll be safe, it'll go away. He wondered if it had mistaken him for some hostile animal, lurking down in the corn.

????
What is the story-line?

????
Who are the main characters?

5 His progress was very slow, through the cornfield, <u>the thick stalks bunched together and got in his way</u>, and he had to shove them back with his arms. But he reached the gate and climbed it, and dropped on to the grass of the field on the other side. Sweat was running down his forehead and into his eyes. <u>He looked up. The crow kept on coming. He ran.</u>

6 But it wasn't easy to run down this field, either, because of the tractor ruts. He began to leap wildly from side to side of them, his legs stretched as far as they could go, and for a short time, it seemed that he did go faster. The crow dived again, and, as it rose, <u>Kingshaw felt the tip of its black wing, beating against his face</u>. He gave a sudden, dry sob. Then his <u>left foot caught in one of the ruts</u> and he keeled over, going down straight forwards.

7 He lay with his face in the coarse grass, panting and sobbing by turns, with the <u>sound of his own blood pumping through his ears.</u> He felt the sun on the back of his neck, and his ankle was wrenched. But he would be able to get up. He raised his head, and wiped two fingers across his face. A streak of blood came off, from where a thistle had scratched him. He got unsteadily to his feet, taking in deep, desperate breaths of the close air. He could not see the crow.

8 But when he began to walk forwards again, it rose up from the grass a little way off, and began to circle and swoop. Kingshaw broke into a run, sobbing and wiping the damp mess of tears and sweat off his face with one hand. There was a blister on his ankle, rubbed raw by the sandal strap. The crow was still quite high, soaring easily, to keep pace with him. Now, he had scrambled over the third gate, and he was in the field next to the one that belonged to Warings. He could see the back of the house, he began to run much faster.

9 This time, he fell and lay completely winded. Through the runnels of sweat and the sticky tufts of his own hair, <u>he could see a figure looking down at him from one of the top windows of the house.</u>

10 Then, there was <u>a single screech, and the terrible beating of wings</u>, and the crow swooped down and landed in the middle of his back.

11 Kingshaw thought that, in the end, it must have been his screaming that frightened it off, for he dared not move. He lay and closed his eyes and felt the claws of the bird, digging into his skin, through the thin shirt, and began to scream in a queer, gasping sort of way. After a moment or two, the bird rose. He had expected it to begin pecking at him with its beak, <u>remembering terrible stories about vultures that went for living people's eyes</u>. He could not believe in his own escape.

????
What is their relationship?

????
Where is it set?

13

PLOT

In this section the story is exciting and <u>dramatic</u>. It is a story of being chased or followed; it is told entirely from the victim's point of view so that the reader can identify closely with him. This section has a double build-up of tension. It builds up to paragraph 6 when the boy falls; we breathe a sigh of relief as the crow disappears. But then tension mounts when it reappears; there is a continued build-up to paragraph 9 when he falls again. This time it is worse because the crow lands on him.

Examiner's Top Tip
If you were writing about this text in an exam you would need to explain how each of these elements is effective.

THE TEXT EXPLAINED

- The writer is trying to create an atmosphere of tension and fear. To look at how this is achieved we should return to the basic elements of fiction described earlier.
<u>Story-line</u>: The boy, Kingshaw, is chased through a cornfield by a crow. He falls and the crow lands on his back. His screams finally scare it away.
<u>Characters/relationship</u>: Kingshaw and the crow; hunter (crow) and hunted (Kingshaw).
<u>Setting</u>: Isolated cornfields.

CHARACTERISATION

- The characterisation of the boy is important because it helps us understand why he is so frightened. He obviously has a powerful imagination: '<u>perhaps this was only the first of a whole battalion of crows</u>' (paragraph 4). He is also presented as being sensitive to what people say and quite easily frightened: '<u>remembering terrible stories about vultures that went for living people's eyes</u>' (paragraph 11).
- '<u>Stupid to be scared of a rotten bird. What could a bird do?</u>' The tone of this suggests that he is angry with himself for being scared. Although he seems to be quite young he is aware of his weaknesses and is critical of them.

RELATIONSHIPS

The relationship between hunter and hunted is developed through the boy's fear. The power of the crow is increased through reference to its size: '<u>enormous, ragged black wings</u>'; '<u>the largest crow he had ever seen</u>'; '<u>the great crow</u>'. There really isn't a relationship as such and this makes the boy seem very isolated.

SETTING

The setting is not the most important element in this piece of writing. The sense of menace is built up through the description of the crow rather than the surroundings. However, there is a sense that the landscape begins to turn against him: 'he felt his own extreme isolation'; 'thick stalks bunched together and got in his way'; 'it wasn't easy to run ... because of the tractor ruts'; 'a thistle scratched him'.

USE OF LANGUAGE

The way that this section is written, the use of language and structure, is what makes it powerful.

Examiner's Top Tip
A key point to think about is how the writer brings the crow to life.

DETAIL
There is extensive detail about the crow, making it seem more real. There is a description of what it sounds like as well as what it looks like. The detailed description of sounds made by the boy and the crow make the reader feel that there is a complete absence of background noise, highlighting his isolation: 'the sound of his own blood pumping through his ears.'

STRUCTURE
The paragraphs in this extract are all quite short; this keeps the story moving at a quick pace. Some sentences are particularly short; this is a device used by writers to build up dramatic tension and suspense: 'He looked up. The crow kept on coming. He ran.'

REPETITION
Minor details become more significant because they are repeated. For example: 'the inside of its mouth was scarlet' (paragraphs 1 and 3). The structure is repetitive: he runs away and falls, then the same thing happens again.

GLOSSARY
Remember to refer to the glossary of literary terms on pages 8–9.

FROM *A KESTREL FOR A KNAVE* BY BARRY HINES

In this extract Mr Sugden is angry with Billy as he believes he let a goal in deliberately at the end of the PE lesson. Billy is made to have a shower before he is allowed to go home.

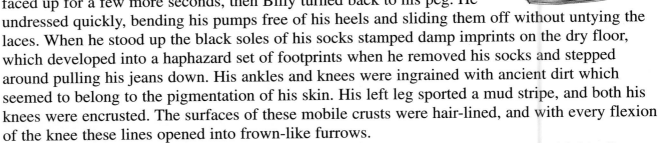

A Kestrel for a Knave

He thought this was funny, Billy didn't. So Sugden looked round for a more appreciative audience. But no one was listening. They faced up for a few more seconds, then Billy turned back to his peg. He undressed quickly, bending his pumps free of his heels and sliding them off without untying the laces. When he stood up the black soles of his socks stamped damp imprints on the dry floor, which developed into a haphazard set of footprints when he removed his socks and stepped around pulling his jeans down. His ankles and knees were ingrained with ancient dirt which seemed to belong to the pigmentation of his skin. His left leg sported a mud stripe, and both his knees were encrusted. The surfaces of these mobile crusts were hair-lined, and with every flexion of the knee these lines opened into frown-like furrows.

For an instant, as he hurried into the showers, with one leg angled in running, with his dirty legs and huge rib cage moulding the skin of his white body, with his hollow cheek in profile, and the sabre of shadow emanating from the eye-hole, just for a moment he resembled an old print of a child hurrying towards the final solution.

****

While he worked on his ankles and heels Sugden stationed three boys at one end of the showers and moved to the other end, where the controls fed into the pipes on the wall … The blunt arrow was pointing to HOT. Sugden swung it back over WARM TO COLD. For a few seconds there was no visible change in the temperature, and the red slice held steady, still dominating the dial. Then it began to recede, slowly at first, then swiftly, its share of the face diminishing rapidly.

The cold water made Billy gasp. He held out his hands as though testing for rain, then ran for the end. The three guards barred the exit.

'Hey up, shift! Let me out, you rotten dogs!' They held him easily so he swished back to the other end, yelling all the way along. Sugden pushed him in the chest as he clung his way round the corner.

'Got a sweat on, Casper?'

'Let me out, Sir. Let me come.'

'I thought you'd like a cooler after your exertions in goal.'

'I'm frozen!'

'Really?'

'Gi' o'er, Sir! It's not right!'

'And was it right when you let the last goal in?'

'I couldn't help it!'

'Rubbish, lad.'

Billy tried another rush. Sugden repelled it, so he tried the other end again. Every time he tried to escape the three boys bounced him back, stinging him with their snapping towels as he retreated. He tried manoeuvring the nozzles, but whichever way he twisted them the water still found him out. Until finally he gave up, and stood amongst them, tolerating the freezing spray in silence. When Billy stopped yelling the other boys stopped laughing, and when time passed and no more was heard from him, their conversations began to peter out, and attention gradually focused on the showers. Until only a trio was left shouting into each other's faces, unaware that the volume of noise in the room had dropped. Suddenly they stopped, looked round embarrassed, then looked towards the showers with the rest of the boys.

The cold water had cooled the air, the steam had vanished, and the only sound that came from the showers was the beat of water behind the partition; a mesmeric beat which slowly drew the boys together on the drying area. The boy guards began to look uneasy, and they looked across to their captain.

'Can we let him out now, Sir?'

'No!'

GLOSSARY
The final solution: During World War Two Hitler and the Nazis decided to kill all Jewish people. Often this was done by gassing in mass showers.

Read the text → Annotate the text → Answer the questions

Plot	Characters	Relationship	Setting

SATS QUESTIONS

1. Look closely at the way the speech is punctuated in this extract.

Which two punctuation marks are most often used to end sentences and what effect does this have?

Punctuation: (1 mark)

Explanation: (1 mark)

2. Look closely at the section beginning _For an instant..._
Explain how this comparison creates sympathy for Billy.

(3 marks)

3. How does the writer show the boys' changing reaction to Billy and how does this increase our sympathy for him? Write your answer on a separate sheet.

Write about:
• **What the boys do and say**
• **the language used to describe their behaviour**
• **the difference between Mr Sugden and the boys** (6 marks)

WHAT TO EXPECT

- Many students think they 'can't do poetry' – they worry about it, perhaps because it is less familiar than other forms of writing. We feel comfortable with fiction, advertising and newspaper reports because we see them around us all the time.
- When trying to understand poetry, it is important to remember that it is simply another means of communicating. A poem is written by another human being wanting to communicate ideas, feelings, memories, hopes and dreams. It may seem less obvious than other forms of writing but this is just because poems are often more compact and less expansive than fiction, for example.

GLOSSARY

As you work through this section remember to refer to the glossary of literary terms on pages 8–9.

POETRY IN SATS

- **Your understanding of poetry might be tested in the Reading section of Paper One in your SATs.**
- **You could be asked to: pick out particular words and phrases and comment on their effectiveness; explain how the structure of the poem adds to the meaning or give a personal response to the poem.**
- **The questions will test your understanding and response to poetry, not your written expression.**

UNDERSTANDING A POEM

TO ACHIEVE LEVEL 5 YOU NEED TO:
- understand what the poem is about
- begin to look for layers of meaning beneath the surface of the text
- understand ideas and feelings in the poem
- notice the effects of particular words and phrases.

TO MOVE FROM LEVEL 5 TO LEVELS 6 AND 7 YOU ALSO NEED TO:
- comment on the effective use of words and phrases and particular devices of language
- locate and comment on the use of imagery
- comment on the structure of the poem
- trace development within a poem
- give a personal response to the poem and what you think the poet has achieved.

READING POETRY

Chaucer SHELLEY
WORDSWORTH t.s eliot
coleridge Keats

By the end of this section you will be able to identify and comment on:

- **title**
- **poetic voice**
- **imagery**
- **language devices**
- **structure**

You should be able to use these elements to make a _personal_ _response_ to poetry.

Examiner's Top Tip
Remember, just like a painting or a piece of music, a poem can be responded to in many different ways. So long as you can justify (back up and explain) your opinion you can't go wrong!

READING THE POEM

- You shouldn't expect to understand everything about a poem after a first reading; it will be packed full of emotions, ideas and images. Reading a poem involves detective work – you have to look closely under the surface for clues.

- Try reading a poem through <u>three</u> times, each time looking for a different set of clues.

Have a go ...
Now read the poem by Seamus Heaney printed on the next page. Read it <u>three</u> times and look for the different clues each time. See if you agree with the ideas on the next page.

First reading: The general meaning and story-line of the poem (if it has one).

Second reading: Feelings and emotions contained in the poem.

Third reading: Interesting <u>images</u> contained in the poem.

DEATH OF A NATURALIST meaning?

time →

All year the flax-dam festered in the heart
Of the townland; green and heavy headed
Flax had rotted there, weighted down by huge sods.
Daily it sweltered in the punishing sun.
Bubbles gargled delicately, bluebottles ← sensory images
Wove a strong gauze of sound around the smell.
There were dragon-flies, spotted butterflies,
But best of all was the warm thick slobber
Of frogspawn that grew like clotted water ← simile
In the shade of the banks. Here, every spring ← time
I would fill jampotsful of the jellied
Specks to range on window-sills at home,
On shelves at school, and wait and watch until
The fattening dots burst into nimble- ← long sentence
Swimming tadpoles. Miss Walls would tell us how
The daddy frog was called a bullfrog
And how he croaked and how the mammy frog } ← voice
Laid hundreds of little eggs and this was
Frogspawn. You could tell the weather by frogs too
For they were yellow in the sun and brown
In rain.

war image

time →

onomatopoeia

Then one hot day when fields were rank
With cowdung in the grass and angry frogs
Invaded the flax-dam; I ducked through hedges
To a coarse croaking that I had not heard
Before. The air was thick with a bass chorus.
Right down the dam gross-bellied frogs were cocked
On sods; their loose necks pulsed like sails. Some hopped
The slap and plop were obscene threats. Some sat
simile → Poised like mud grenades, their blunt heads farting.
war image I sickened, turned, and ran. The great slime kings ← comic book image
Were gathered there for vengeance and I knew
short sentence That if I dipped my hand the spawn would clutch it.

Seamus Heaney

Examiner's Top Tip
Making notes or annotating a poem (underlining and highlighting, etc.) is a helpful way of organising your thoughts about it.

1ST READING

The poem is about a young boy (the poet) interested in nature, particularly frogspawn; he collects it and watches it grow. One day he is frightened by the frogs; he imagines they are going to attack him. He runs away; this ends his interest in nature.

2ND READING

Stanza One: fascination with nature and wildlife; excitement waiting for hatching; fond memories of childhood
Stanza Two: fear of big frogs; revulsion at their appearance; terror and hatred

3RD READING

"bubbles gargled delicately"; "gauze of sound"; "clotted water"; images of war; "The great slime kings"

TIME

The references to time in this poem are very interesting. In the first stanza all the times are general: 'All year', 'every spring'. The first stanza describes a general interest in nature. It also shows that the collecting of frogspawn is something he does every year and that he is very familiar with the area he describes, having visited it often: 'Daily it sweltered...' The reference to time in the second stanza is a signpost for the move from general enjoyment to a specific event at a specific point in time: 'Then one hot day...'.

DEATH OF A NATURALIST: THE TEXT EXPLAINED

SIMILES

If you pick out similes you must also explain why they are effective. For example: 'poised like mud grenades'. This shows that the poet found them threatening and unpredictable, likely to explode (jump) at any time. It also reflects the colour and shape of the frogs.

WAR IMAGES

Notice the use of words connected to war in the second stanza. The young boy feels as though the frogs have formed an army to fight back against the theft of frogspawn. He feels as if he's about to be ambushed: 'I ducked through hedges'.

COMIC BOOK IMAGE

'The great slime kings' are the product of a young child's overactive imagination just like monsters that hide under your bed! Where the first stanza contained sophisticated language and images from adulthood, this seems to come straight out of a nightmare or a comic strip, reflecting the raw terror felt at the time. He doesn't think the spawn might clutch his hand, he knows.

ONOMATOPOEIA

Words like 'slap' and 'plop' give his writing immediacy because they make the reader feel as if they can hear the threatening sounds that the young boy heard.

Examiner's Top Tip
If you are using technical terms from the glossary, make sure you spell them correctly.

TITLE: DEATH OF A NATURALIST

The title is confusing; we expect to read about a death, instead we find the story of a young boy's fascination with frogspawn. As we read on we discover that the death is not literal (real), it is symbolic (represents something else). A naturalist is a person who is interested in nature and wildlife, the young boy in this case; the death is of his interest in nature. After the encounter with the frogs he is no longer a naturalist. This poem is about 'rites of passage', the move from childhood into adulthood. The poem could also symbolise the 'death' of childhood innocence. The innocent view of the goodness of nature is destroyed, never to be regained.

POETIC VOICE

Most of the poem is written in **voice of the poet** remembering his youth, but lines 16–19 are the **voice of Miss Walls**, his primary school teacher. The change of voice adds variety and also shows that these words have stayed in his memory. The **vocabulary** is more childish; '**the mammy frog**'. This provides a contrast to the more sophisticated language used earlier in the stanza, e.g. '**bubbles gargled delicately**'.

SENSORY IMAGES

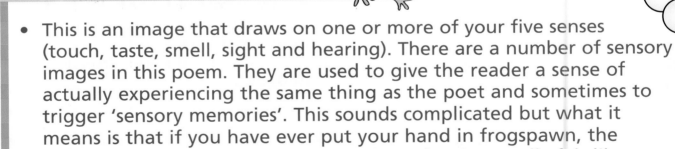

- This is an image that draws on one or more of your five senses (touch, taste, smell, sight and hearing). There are a number of sensory images in this poem. They are used to give the reader a sense of actually experiencing the same thing as the poet and sometimes to trigger 'sensory memories'. This sounds complicated but what it means is that if you have ever put your hand in frogspawn, the description should make you remember what it actually felt like.
- To move up a level (level 6/7), try to think of other reasons why sensory images may have been used. For example, he is writing about childhood experiences. Children learn through their senses – every new sound, smell and taste is remembered. The 'warm thick slobber/Of frogspawn' is, perhaps, connected to a memory of a dog licking a hand or face!
- Think about the language used to express these images. For example: 'bubbles gargled delicately' – this is not the language of a young child. It shows that this is a mature adult fondly remembering, perhaps romanticising, his past. You could perhaps try to explain the contradictions of 'gauze of sound' and 'clotted water'. Why did he use these images?

THE POEM EXPLAINED

You shouldn't feel daunted by such a detailed explanation of the poem. It covers most of the elements that you could pick out of the text. You would not be expected to write at such length.

SENTENCE STRUCTURE

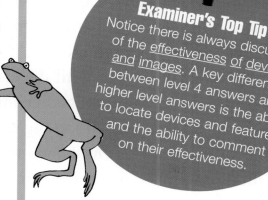

- In the second stanza sentences are quite short, particularly the one highlighted: 'I sickened, turned, and ran.' Short sentences are used to build up dramatic tension and suspense. This sentence comes as the threats have built to a peak and the young boy decides to run away. This sentence is broken into even shorter units by the use of commas, giving a moment's pause for thought before each action. This use of short sentences is in contrast to the rambling 34-word sentence in the first stanza. To best understand the effect of the sentence which begins: 'Here, every spring' you should go back to it and read it out loud.

- You should be feeling slightly out of breath now! As you read that section of the poem you find yourself speeding up to fit all the words in before you run out of breath. This is intended to reflect the excitement and anticipation of 'watching and waiting' for the hatching of the frogspawn. It also copies the final burst into life described at the end of the sentence. The technique of enjambment keeps the poem moving forward rather than breaking up the action with unnecessary commas and full stops.

Examiner's Top Tip
Notice there is always discussion of the effectiveness of devices and images. A key difference between level 4 answers and higher level answers is the ability to locate devices and features and the ability to comment on their effectiveness.

Examiner's Top Tip
Remember to read to the punctuation. In other words, only take a breath when there is a punctuation mark.

ADVICE

Go back to the poem and the explanations and pick out those parts with which you feel most comfortable, then try to look for those elements in other poems that you read. Build up gradually, looking for different elements each time you read.

THE BASIC AREAS COVERED ARE:

- ❖ title
- ❖ imagery
- ❖ language devices
- ❖ poetic voice
- ❖ structure
- ❖ personal response

Blackberry Picking

Late August, given heavy rain and sun
For a full week, the blackberries would ripen.
At first, just one, a glossy purple clot
Among others, red, green, hard as a knot.
You ate the first one and its flesh was sweet
Like thickened wine: summer's blood was in it
Leaving stains upon the tongue and lust for
Picking. Then red ones inked up and that hunger
Sent us out with milk-cans, pea-tins, jam-pots
Where briars scratched and wet grass bleached our boots.
Round hayfields, cornfields and potato drills
We trekked and picked until the cans were full,
Until the tinkling bottom had been covered
With green ones, and on top big dark blobs burned
Like a plate of eyes. Our hands were peppered
With thorn pricks, our palms sticky as Bluebeard's.

We hoarded the fresh berries in the byre.
But when the bath was filled we found a fur,
A rat-grey fungus glutting on our cache.
The juice was stinking too. Once off the bush
The fruit fermented, the sweet flesh would turn sour.
I always felt like crying. It wasn't fair
That all the lovely canfuls smelt of rot.
Each year I hoped they would keep, knew they would not.

Seamus Heaney

GLOSSARY

Bluebeard: A pirate who killed many of his wives by chopping off their heads.
Byre: A cowshed.
Cache: A hidden store of treasure, provisions or weapons.

<u>Read</u> the poem three times → <u>Annotate</u> the poem ↓ <u>Answer</u> the questions

1st READING
The story-line

2nd READING
Feelings and emotions in the poem

3rd READING
Interesting images and phrases

SATS QUESTIONS

1. Find and copy a simile used in the first stanza and explain why it is effective.

Simile:

Explanation: (2 marks)

2. Find and copy two words in the second stanza which link to *Bluebeard* **in the first stanza. Explain why the poet has used the image these words help to create.**

Words used:

Explanation: (3 marks)

3. Look closely at the section beginning *Then red ones inked up* **... and ending ...** *Like a plate of eyes.* **How does the sentence structure and the choice of vocabulary help to create a sense of the children's movement?**

Sentence structure: (2 marks)

Vocabulary: (2 marks)

READING A NON-FICTION TEXT

There are many different types of non-fiction text and they all follow different rules and conventions. The main non-fiction types are:

- instruction
- information
- persuasion
- recount
- explanation
- discursive.

On this page you will find a brief description of the convention of each text.

INSTRUCTION

Purpose: to instruct how something should be done through a series of sequenced steps.

STRUCTURE
A statement of what is to be achieved.
List of materials and equipment.
Sequenced/chronological steps.
Sometimes a diagram or illustration.

LANGUAGE
Written in the imperative
– tells you what
to do.

INFORMATION

Purpose: to describe the way things are; to give information.

STRUCTURE
Information is clearly organised
Information is linked.
Examples are included.

LANGUAGE
Present tense
Written in the third
person: he, she, it

UNDERSTANDING NON-FICTION

TO ACHIEVE LEVEL 5 YOU NEED TO:
- find information and ideas in a text
- show a basic understanding of the text
- note the use of particular words and phrases
- be aware of why a text has been written.

TO MOVE FROM LEVEL 5 TO LEVELS 6 AND 7 YOU ALSO NEED TO:
- comment on use of language and layout (if appropriate)
- show awareness of what the writer is trying to achieve and how they do it
- say how successful you think the writer has been
- give a personal response to the text.

PERSUASION

<u>Purpose:</u>
to persuade or to argue the case for a point of view

STRUCTURE
Opening statement: E.g. vegetables are good for you.
Persuasive argument – point plus support.
Summary of argument and restatement of opening.

LANGUAGE
Present tense
Logical connectives

RECOUNT

<u>Purpose:</u> to retell event

STRUCTURE
An opening which sets the scene.
Events are retold in chronological order.

LANGUAGE
Written in the past tense
Uses temporal connectives: then, next, after
Focuses on individuals or groups of people: I, we

Examiner's Top Tip
When you are writing a non-fiction text make sure you follow these conventions.

Examiner's Top Tip
These conventions are not a rigid set of rules – they are intended as a guide. Many texts are mixed text types.

EXPLANATION

<u>Purpose:</u> to explain the process involved in natural and social phenomena or to explain how something works.

STRUCTURE
A statement to introduce the topic.
A series of logical steps explaining how and why something happens.
Steps continue until explanation is complete.

LANGUAGE
Present tense
Logical connectives:
  this shows, because
Temporal connectives:
  then, next, later

DISCURSIVE

<u>Purpose:</u> to present arguments and information rom differing viewpoints.

STRUCTURE
Statement of the issue to be discussed.
Argument for plus supporting evidence.
Argument against plus supporting evidence.
Summary of arguments and recommendation.

LANGUAGE
Present tense
Logical connectives:
therefore, however

AUTOBIOGRAPHY

A <u>personal</u> <u>life</u> <u>story</u>. The author selects and reconstructs events from their own life to share with the public. We should remember when reading an autobiography that no one has total recall of their entire life and a personal account of the subject's own life is bound to be biased. The events from a person's past are, of course, recounted with hindsight, allowing us to see the lessons that have been learned from those events.

Based on fact

A non-fiction text is something that is <u>based</u> on fact or involves a true story. However, the boundaries between fiction and non-fiction are becoming more and more blurred. There have always been historical novels to read but now we are able to watch 'docu-soaps' on television and new words like 'faction' and 'news fiction' have become commonplace media terms.

READING NON-FICTION

The kind of non-fiction texts that you might expect to find in your test are:

- autobiography
- biography
- media
- diaries
- letters
- travel writing

On this spread you will find a brief explanation about why they are written and what to look for in each.

BIOGRAPHY

A written account of a person's life, written by someone else. There are two kinds of <u>biography</u>: <u>authorised</u> and <u>unauthorised</u>.

AUTHORISED

An <u>authorised</u> biographer has the permission of the subject to write their life story. Often the biographer will have been asked by the subject to write about them and may have spent many hours discussing the events to be included. This will affect the way they recount particular events.

UNAUTHORISED

<u>Unauthorised</u> <u>biographies</u> are written without the permission of the subject. They are generally thought to be less <u>reliable</u>. The biographer relies on information from people who know the subject and from more widely available sources. Some might claim that this kind of biography could be more accurate, as the writer is under no obligation to hide anything that could be embarrassing or damaging.

MEDIA

See <u>Media</u> <u>section</u> on pages 36–45.

DIARIES

Maybe you keep a diary or a journal. Would you like thousands of people to read it? Diaries are a record of <u>personal</u> <u>thoughts</u>, <u>feelings</u>, <u>hopes</u> and <u>dreams</u>. One of the most famous and widely read diaries is that of <u>Anne</u> <u>Frank</u>. Her father allowed its publication after her death in a concentration camp. Her writings have been an inspiration to people all over the world. When we read a diary we should always remember that it is an <u>intensely</u> <u>personal</u> <u>document</u>, not at all like a biography that was always intended for publication.

LETTERS

Like diaries, private letters are personal documents not initially intended for publication. Public letters, written for newspapers or widespread circulation are, of course, very different and may aim to <u>persuade</u> us of something or change our opinions.

TRAVEL WRITING

Although people have long been fascinated with travel, travel writing is a newly popular genre. It is as much about people and personal struggle as it is about the places they have travelled to. Travel writing is often designed to <u>entertain</u> as well as <u>inform</u>. This form of writing can be compared with diaries, as accounts of journeys often begin as personal journals.

Biased text

Remember that texts written by one person about their own personal experiences are bound to be <u>biased</u>. Some elements may be given more emphasis whilst others are hardly mentioned. As you develop your understanding of non-fiction texts, <u>a key skill will be the ability to recognise when you, as a reader, are being manipulated</u>. It is important to try to keep the facts in mind, to take a balanced view and to work out exactly what the writer wants you to think and feel. As you improve your reading skills you will find it easier to do this and to see how and why a writer achieves his or her aims.

Basic questions

When you read a non-fiction text, begin by asking yourself four basic questions.

<u>Who</u> **is it aimed at?**

<u>Why</u> **has it been written?**

<u>What</u> **is the main idea/message in the text?**

<u>How</u> **is that message put across?**

READING NON-FICTION: EXAMPLE TEXT

This extract is from Nelson Mandela's autobiography *Long Walk to Freedom*. He writes about his rural African upbringing; his struggle against apartheid; his imprisonment and finally his election as President of South Africa. This extract is from the section entitled 'Robben Island: the dark years'. In it he describes his prison life.

Look for the conventions of recount:

- Retells events in chronological order
- Uses temporal connectives
- Written in the past tense
- Focuses on individuals or identified groups

See pages 32–33 where the text is explained.

THE TEXT

Long Walk to Freedom

In the midst of breakfast, the guards would yell, "Val in! Val in!" (Fall in! Fall in!), and we would stand outside our cells for inspection. Each prisoner was required to have the three buttons of his khaki jacket properly buttoned. We were required to doff our hats as the warder walked by. If our buttons were undone, our hats unremoved, or our cells untidy, we were charged with a violation of the prison code and punished with either solitary confinement or the loss of meals.

After inspection we would work in the courtyard hammering stones until noon. There were no breaks; if we slowed down the warders would yell at us to speed up. At noon, the bell would clang for lunch and another metal drum of food would be wheeled into the courtyard. For Africans, lunch consisted of boiled mealies, that is, coarse kernels of corn. The Indians and Coloured prisoners received samp, or mealie rice, which consisted of ground mealies in a soup-like mixture. The samp was sometimes served with vegetables, whereas our mealies were served straight.

For lunch we often received *phuzamandla*, which means 'drink of strength', a powder made from mealies and a bit of yeast. It is meant to be stirred into water or milk, and when it is thick it can be tasty, but the prison authorities gave us so little of the powder that it barely coloured the water. I would

????
Who **is it aimed at?**

????
Why **has it been written?**

usually save my powder for several days until I had enough to make a proper drink, but if the authorities discovered you were hoarding food, the powder was confiscated and you were punished.

After lunch we worked until 4, when the guards blew shrill whistles and we once again lined up to be counted and inspected. We were then permitted half an hour to clean up. The bathroom at the end of our corridor had two seawater showers, a saltwater tap and three large galvanized metal buckets, which were used as bathtubs. There was no hot water. We would stand or squat in these buckets, soaping ourselves with the brackish water, rinsing off the dust from the day. To wash yourself with cold water when it is cold outside is not pleasant, but we made the best of it. We would sometimes sing while washing, which made the water seem less icy. In those early days, this was one of the only times when we could converse.

Precisely at 4.30 there would be a loud knock on the wooden door at the end of the corridor, which meant that supper had been delivered. Common-law prisoners used to dish out the food to us and we would return to our cells to eat it. We again received mealie pap porridge, sometimes with the odd carrot or piece of cabbage or beetroot thrown in – but one usually had to search for it. If we did get a vegetable, we would usually have the same one for weeks on end, until the cabbage or carrots were old and mouldy and we thoroughly sick of them. Every other day we received a small piece of meat with our porridge. The meat was mostly gristle.

For supper, Coloured and Indian prisoners received a quarter loaf of bread (known as *katkopf*, that is, a cat's head, after the shape of the bread) and a slab of margarine. Africans, it was presumed, did not care for bread as it was a 'European' type of food.

Typically, we received even less than the scanty amounts stipulated in the regulations. This was because the kitchen was rife with smuggling. The cooks – all of whom were common-law prisoners – kept the best food for themselves or their friends. Often they would lay aside the tastiest morsel for the warders in exchange for favours or preferential treatment.

At 8 p.m. the night warder would lock himself in the corridor with us, passing the key through a small hole in the door to another warder outside. The warder would then walk up and down the corridor, ordering us to go to sleep. No cry of 'lights out' was ever given on Robben Island because the single mesh-covered bulb in our cell burned day and night. Later, those studying for higher degrees were permitted to read until 10 or 11 p.m.

????
What is the main idea/message in the text?

????
How is that message put across?

Who?
It is aimed at people interested in politics; apartheid and the struggle against it; general interest, Mandela being a well-known figure around the world.

Why?
To maintain the author's sense of identity in times of trouble (much of it was written whilst still in prison). To make people aware of the struggle against apartheid and how people suffered. To make sure people don't forget how things were and to ensure more progress is made.

Examiner's Top Tip
In your tests you will be instructed to 'refer to words and phrases to back up your ideas'.

How?
A factual and detailed account told without emotion; comparisons of food to highlight prejudice.

What?
The harshness of the regime; prejudice in the prison; that it is possible to survive such hardship with dignity.

RELATIONSHIPS

The writer has used this book as a way of communicating with others. This extract shows that communication with other prisoners was rare: 'In those early days, this was one of the only times we could converse.' This extract also shows that relationships with the guards were poor: 'In the midst of 'breakfast ... Val in! Val in!'; 'the guards blew shrill whistles'; 'a loud knock on the wooden door'; 'ordering us to go to sleep'. All of these quotations show that there was no conversation between prisoners and guards, just the shouting of orders.

FOOD

Examiner's Top Tip
All of these comments are backed up with direct quotation or close reference to the text.

All of the prison meals are described in detail. Each time there is a description of the differences in rations for Black prisoners and Coloured and Indian prisoners. This is done to highlight prejudice in the system. 'The samp was sometimes served with vegetables, whereas our mealies were served straight.'

SANITATION

Arrangements for washing are described in great detail, again done to highlight how poor the conditions were.

THE TEXT EXPLAINED

This description of daily routine is used to show that basic human rights were only just attended to in this prison. It also clearly shows that the system was run on prejudice. That is the main message of the text – now we need to look more closely at how it is put across to the reader.

ROUTINE

There are many references to time in this extract and meals are described in great detail. This indicates the daily routine was important, perhaps for keeping track of time. It also shows that there was little of interest happening in normal days.

Does the writer find routine a comfort?

COPING STRATEGIES

There are some clues in this extract as to how the prisoners coped with the harsh regime. They are to do with communication and stimulating the brain: 'We would sometimes sing while washing, which made the water seem less icy.'

TONE

Although the writer is describing a 'dark time' in his life, the tone is very matter-of-fact and not at all self-pitying or exaggerated. This makes the reader more inclined to believe that the details are true and the harshness of his existence has not been dramatised for impact.

PUNISHMENT

In this extract punishments are not described but it is made clear that minor offences are punished severely: 'If our buttons were undone ... punished with either solitary confinement or the loss of meals.'

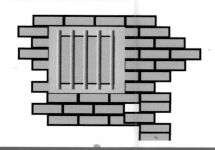

Recount text conventions
- Autobiographies follow many of the text conventions of a recount.
- Retells events in chronological order: this extract details a day in prison from breakfast to bedtime.
- Uses temporal connectives: 'After inspection ...', 'At 8 p.m....'
- Written in past tense: 'For lunch we often received'
- Focuses on individuals or identified groups: 'the guards would yell', 'we worked until 4'

This extract is from a piece of travel writing *On Foot Through Africa*
by Ffyona Cambell. Here she describes part of her journey through Zaire.
Villagers were often hostile, fearing that she was involved in the slave trade.
Although she made the journey alone and on foot, she did have two back-up
drivers, Bill and Blake, who feature in this passage.

On Foot Through Africa

1 It was the constant focus of their attention. The boys went ahead through one village
and I passed along ten minutes later to find the people still standing together in the
centre staring after them. I came behind them, a white, undefended, feeling like a
beetle walking into a dawn patrol of ants. An old man broke the silence with a
barrage of shrill words. The crowd broke and re-formed around me, their shrill
whooping getting louder and louder until it was a throbbing wall of sound. I daren't
turn. I walked out of the village and I waved goodbye. Ten minutes later the hill
behind was teeming with bands of children, whooping and hollering, their demands
growing louder and louder. The tension needed relieving so I turned and smiled.
They closed around me, getting excited. The ringleader grabbed at my necklace,
demanding to know what it was.

2 'It is a present from my husband,' I said. 'Thank you for escorting me to him – he
is waiting ahead.' And luckily both of them were.
Getting into camp was a relief not just because it meant I was safe but because I
was not the only thing they were baiting any more.

3 A couple of the boys would arrive first to watch the camp from a distance. Then
more would come, just standing a small distance away. As the group grew, they
merged into a crowd and became cocky. They were kids who'd found a new toy,
and they loved to bait, to mess about with it to see what it would do. They did this
to me on the road – imitating me, shouting at me, and then a stone would be
thrown. Blake had to diffuse this in camp; I had to defuse this on the road. In camp,
we could usually get them to leave in the early stages by picking out one and staring at him – this made them very self-conscious and they'd turn and leave.

4 On the road, I would turn and suddenly growl with my hands out like claws. The
children would scatter like impala changing direction. Some would take a look
back at a distance when they saw me laughing, they would laugh too and run back
to hold my hand and dance along. But, after a short while, they wanted to do it
again – as kids do – and the group would be gradually replaced as I walked through a
long village, kids getting bored with it and falling back, to be replaced with new
ones who started the baiting again.

5 The young teenage girls were the worst – they imitated my gait and would not
respond to my games or return my smiles; they just sniggered. Teenage girls are
the same the world over. There were times when I couldn't get the kids to laugh,
possibly because I wasn't exuding the right presence. Then the stoning would be

vicious. It is humiliating to be stoned, to be physically and symbolically chased out. I couldn't run; I couldn't stop them by stoning them back; I couldn't reason with them; I couldn't often get the adults to help. I was crying inside. Sometimes they hollered like Red Indians, a disorientating sound that made me feel like a hunted animal. I wondered if it was, indeed, a form of hunting. I hummed a Vangelis tune to make me feel like I wasn't actually there, just watching myself in a movie.

Read the text   Annotate the text   Answer the questions

Who?	Why?	What?	How?

SATS QUESTIONS

1. Find and copy a simile in the first paragraph. Explain why it is effective.

Simile:

Explanation: (1 mark)

2. In the final paragraph, the phrase *I couldn't* is repeated several times in one sentence. What is the effect of this?

(2 marks)

3. After reading the whole passage, what impressions do you get about the writer's relationship with the villagers? Write your answer on a separate sheet.

Write about:
• The way she describes their behaviour
• The use of language and imagery
• Your personal response to the text

NEWSPAPER

Aim: to inform, entertain, change opinion
Layout: headline, columns, short paragraphs, pictures
Language: should be factual though some articles contain bias and opinion, Standard English, headlines use alliteration, puns, etc.

LEAFLET

Aim: to give information or advice on a particular topic; to <u>persuade</u> the reader to change their opinion; to help the reader
Layout: different font styles and sizes, headings, columns, bullet points, pictures/ graphs and charts
Language: Standard English, fact and opinion, simple sentence structure and vocabulary choices to reach a wider audience

Examiner's Top Tip
Always explain <u>why</u> and <u>how</u> language devices and layout have been used.

UNDERSTANDING A MEDIA TEXT

TO ACHIEVE LEVEL 5 YOU NEED TO:
- be able to <u>locate information</u> and ideas in the text
- be aware of the <u>purpose</u> of the text
- note the importance of <u>layout features</u>
- note the use of <u>particular words and phrases</u>.

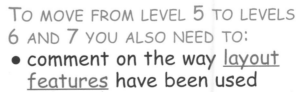

TO MOVE FROM LEVEL 5 TO LEVELS 6 AND 7 YOU ALSO NEED TO:
- comment on the way <u>layout features</u> have been used
- comment on the way particular <u>language devices</u> have been used
- say how successful the writer has been in achieving their purpose
- give a <u>personal response</u> to the text.

ADVERTISEMENT

WE CLEAN 'EM

OH BOY! IT LOOKS NEW!

<u>Aim</u>: to attract attention; to <u>inform</u>; to <u>persuade</u> reader to buy a product or service

<u>Layout</u>: lots of pictures, different font sizes and styles, bright colours, small blocks of text, slogans and captions

<u>Language</u>: emotive and persuasive, slogans use alliteration, puns, questions and repetition, more opinion than fact, sometimes use slang expressions

READING MEDIA TEXTS

Media texts are mostly intended to <u>persuade</u>.
They aim to persuade us:
- **to buy something**
- **to do something**
- **to change our opinion about something**

In the case of newspapers they also aim to inform us and perhaps entertain us.

In your exam you might expect to find these media texts:
- **newspaper article**
- **information/advice leaflet**
- **advertisement**
- **holiday brochure**
- **letter from a charity**

Examiner's Top Tip
Look on the next spread pages 38–39 for more detailed explanations of language and layout devices.

CHARITY LETTER

<u>Aim</u>: to <u>persuade</u> the reader to give money or get involved in a project

<u>Layout</u>: short paragraphs, standard letter layout, bold type, tear-off sections, pictures

<u>Language</u>: Standard English, emotive language, fact and opinion

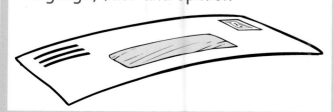

HOLIDAY BROCHURE

<u>Aim</u>: to <u>persuade</u> the reader to buy a holiday

<u>Layout</u>: lots of pictures, tables and charts, short block of text, different font sizes

<u>Language</u>: emotive and persuasive, fact and opinion, descriptions in note form often using abbreviations

GREAT AMERICAN SPRING AND SUMMERTIME TOURS

GLOSSARY OF MEDIA TERMS

Later in this section, you will find some examples of how to comment on these features in an exam. If you can locate these features you can hope to achieve level 5. However, you must say how and why these features are used to achieve level 6 or higher.

NEWSPAPER

Broadsheet: A newspaper, considered to be more factual and serious than a tabloid. Aims to inform and report, not to entertain. Broadsheets are the larger of the two newspaper styles. Examples: The Guardian and The Times.

Columns: Newspaper and magazine articles are set out in columns; leaflets sometimes use this format too. Columns break up a page and make it more interesting to look at.

Headlines: In newspapers they are particularly important attention grabbers. They are made deliberately dramatic so that the audience will read on. In tabloid newspapers headlines are often linked to pictures to make up the majority of the front page. Language devices such as alliteration, rhyme and repetition are often used.

Pictures: In newspapers they are used to back up and dramatise or personalise a story – they are often closely linked with headlines.

Quotations: A direct comment taken from someone involved in the newspaper story. This gives the report validity and can often give a more personalised feel. Reporters are required to be unbiased and give a balanced account of the story, but the people involved will often be on one side or another.

Short paragraphs: Long paragraphs can be off-putting for a busy reader. Most media texts are organised into short paragraphs to hold attention.

Tabloid: This kind of newspaper is considered to be less serious and, sometimes, less factual than a broadsheet. As well as reporting, these papers also aim to entertain. Examples: The Sun and The Mirror.

Topic sentence: The first sentence of a newspaper story, closely linked to the headline. It usually tells you who, what, when and where the story happened.

OTHER TERMS

Audience: The readership that a text is aimed at. In advertising, a lot of market research is done so that products can be aimed at very specific groups of people.

Tone of voice: This often indicates the emotions and feelings that the writer wishes to put across to the reader. Examples of tone of voice could be persuasive, conversational, informative, tempting, dramatic or conspiratorial. You would not expect the tone to be aggressive or superior as this would put the reader off.

LEAFLET

<u>Bold</u> <u>print</u>: Darker print makes important information stand out from the rest of the text.

<u>Bullet</u> <u>points</u>: Often marked out with an asterisk or small symbol, these short sentences or phrases attract the attention of the busy reader.

<u>Font</u> <u>styles</u>: Different styles of printing are used to make text look different or attractive. Sometimes a particular font may be used to link it to the subject of the text.

<u>Frames</u> <u>and</u> <u>borders</u>: Sections of text may be boxed in to highlight their importance or to group together text that covers the same topic.

<u>Graphs</u> <u>and</u> <u>charts</u>: Used to demonstrate the facts in a clear visual way; they can be used to back up claims made in text and can be quite dramatic.

<u>Pictures</u>: In leaflets they can be emotive: a picture of a lonely pensioner or a starving African child.

<u>Subheadings</u>: Are like signposts to the important information in any text. Key words and phrases are picked out to focus the reader's attention.

ADVERTISEMENT

<u>Personal</u> <u>pronouns</u>: In persuasive writing, particularly advertising, the pronouns **you** and **we** are used extensively. This is to make the reader feel that they are being addressed individually and personally. This also works in charity appeals. E.g. **You** could make a difference if **you** give just £5.

<u>Pictures</u>: In advertising, the picture can be more important than the text. They can be tempting and colourful or more stylised, perhaps black and white.

<u>Slogans</u>: Main use is in advertising. It is a 'catchphrase' linked to the product, aimed to stick in the minds of the target audience. Slogans make use of language devices such as: <u>alliteration</u>, e.g. The Totally Tropical Taste; <u>repetition</u>, e.g. Have a break. Have a Kit Kat;

WE CLEAN 'EM
OH BOY! IT LOOKS NEW!

<u>puns</u>, e.g. Bakers born and bread, and <u>questions</u>, e.g. Have **you** had **your** Weetabix? <u>Text</u> <u>size</u>: Important information is in larger print; less appealing information – terms and conditions, for example – tend to be smaller.

SOME EXAMPLES OF THE DIFFERENT STYLES USED FOR MAKING LEAFLETS

EXAMPLES OF DIFFERENT styles used for creating a leaflet.

Examples of different styles used for creating a leaflet. Examples of different styles.

used for creating a leaflet. Examples of different styles used for creating a leaflet

Have a go ...
Try to identify some of these features in media texts you find at home and in school.

READING A MEDIA TEXT

Study this leaflet very carefully. It was produced by a leading supermarket chain to encourage healthy eating. Look closely at the annotated sections and see if you can work out how each of these details would back up your answers to the four basic questions.

See pages 42–43 where the text is explained.

Headings: break up the text and draw your attention to important information

Columns: break up the text and make it easier to scan

Bullet points: show the important information in quick note form

Slogan: short and snappy; use of exclamation mark

Healthy Eating with Fruit and Vegetables

If you have been put off changing the way you eat because healthy eating advice in the past has told you what you should not eat, here's the good news. There are many delicious foods that you can eat more of - fruit and vegetables.

Fruit and vegetables are full of vitamins, minerals and fibre which are needed to maintain good health. They are also very low in fat.

Experts agree a diet low in fat and rich in fruit and vegetables (as well as starchy foods such as potatoes, bread, pasta, rice and other cereals), is best for health. So eating more fruit and vegetables helps you gain a healthier balance of foods.

Servings

Five servings can easily fit into a normal day's eating as shown below.
Don't count potatoes in your five-a-day total because although it is a good idea to eat more of them, they are classified as starchy foods along with pasta, bread, rice and other cereals.

Breakfast - glass of unsweetened fruit juice (which counts as a serving of fruit), and/or fresh fruit chopped onto your breakfast cereal = 1-2 servings

Mid-morning - fruit instead of biscuits or confectionery = 1 serving

Lunch - salad or vegetables with your meal, or fruit instead of pudding = 1-2 servings

Evening meal - as for lunch = 1-2 servings
1 serving equals:
- 2 tablespoons vegetables
- small salad
- piece fresh fruit
- 2 tablespoons stewed or canned fruit
- glass (100ml) fruit juice

Five-a-Day!

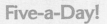

Most people need to double the amount of fruit and vegetables they eat, whether it be fresh, frozen or canned (without added sugar or salt) to about 400g (1lb) in order to strike the right balance. Increasing the amount has never been easier because the choice in store has never been wider. There are fruit and vegetables to suit all tastes, occasions and styles of cooking. **The easiest way to eat enough fruit and vegetables is to adopt the Five-a-Day rule.**

????
Who is it aimed at?

????
Why has it been written?

Take 5!
Healthy Eating with Fruit and Vegetables

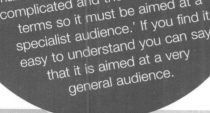
Snack happy

Many people complain that it is difficult to snack healthily, but fruit in particular is the ultimate convenience or 'fast' food because much of it can be enjoyed raw and it comes wrapped in its own neat package. It doesn't take a minute to unzip a banana, which makes an excellent snack for all ages. Ring the changes by choosing fruit in season like peaches, plums and nectarines in the summer and clementines in the winter. Try dried fruit for a change- it makes an excellent snack.

- Add sliced and grated vegetables to sandwich fillings - especially good in toasted sandwiches.
- Add grated vegetables to the meat in cottage and shepherd's pie.
- Mix mashed swede and carrot with mashed potato.
- Mix mashed or puréed fruit with yogurt or fromage frais for a quick dessert.

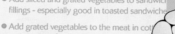

Children's choice

Give children a taste for vegetables and fruit early on to establish good eating habits for life.

- Fruit and vegetable purées are a good basis for weaning foods.
- Add grated carrots or chopped celery and other vegetables to mince when making home-made burgers.
- Use brightly coloured vegetables like tomatoes and sweetcorn to make funny faces on pizza bases.
- Dried fruit like raisins make useful snacks.
- Use fresh or canned fruit in fruit jellies.

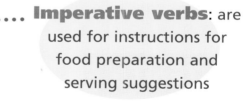

Imperative verbs: are used for instructions for food preparation and serving suggestions

Pictures make the fruit and vegetables look tasty and convenient to eat

????
What is the main idea/message in the text?

????
How is that message put across?

Who
The leaflet is aimed at supermarket shoppers; people who want to diet or start a healthier lifestyle; people who are concerned about what their children eat.

Why
It has been written to encourage people to eat more fruit and vegetables; to promote good health habits and to persuade shoppers to buy fruit and vegetable products from that supermarket.

How
The text is full of straight-forward advice about what to eat. The presentation is simple and attractive.

What
The main idea is that buying and eating more fruit and vegetables will improve your health.

THE TEXT EXPLAINED

This leaflet really has two main purposes. Although it is presented as an advice leaflet about healthy eating, it is also unmistakably an <u>advertisement</u> for the products available in the supermarket. To judge its success, we need to look closely at the content, language and layout of this leaflet.

CONTENT

- There is a balance of <u>facts</u> <u>and</u> <u>opinion</u>, allowing the writer to give factual information but to be persuasive at the same time: '<u>fruit</u> <u>and</u> <u>vegetables</u> <u>are</u> <u>full</u> <u>of</u> <u>minerals</u>', '<u>Try</u> <u>dried</u> <u>fruit</u> <u>for</u> <u>a</u> <u>change</u> – <u>it</u> <u>makes</u> <u>an</u> <u>excellent</u> <u>snack</u>.'
- There are 'expert opinions' to make people believe that the information is medically sound.
- There is an easily achievable target: '<u>adopt</u> <u>the</u> <u>Five-a-Day</u> <u>rule</u>' with information on how to meet the target.
- There are recipe suggestions for making fruit and vegetables more appealing to children.

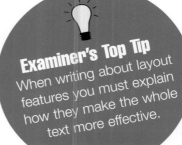

Examiner's Top Tip
When writing about layout features you must explain how they make the whole text more effective.

LANGUAGE

- **The language is straightforward and easy to understand. This is because it is aimed at ordinary shoppers and not a specialist interest group. The language in a healthy-eating leaflet for doctors would probably contain lots of medical terms.**
- **It is written in Standard English so that English-speaking shoppers can understand.**
- **The tone of voice is informal – conversational and friendly. Although it is telling people to change their eating habits it doesn't come across as being overly instructive in tone.**
- **There are suggestions rather than orders: 'Try dried fruit...'. The 'Children's Choice' section is written in the imperative because it is telling you how to serve the food in the same way a recipe would. 'Add grated vegetables', 'Mix mashed or pureed fruit...'**
- **The slogan is catchy and familiar: 'Take 5!' This is usually connected to taking a break or relaxing so it is a 'friendly' term. When you read the rest of the leaflet you realise it is connected to the target 'Five-a-Day rule'.**

LAYOUT

A variety of layout features are used in this leaflet.

Pictures: the front cover is a full-page picture of fruit and vegetables. It looks fresh, healthy and attractive. Inside there are a number of colourful pictures which break up the text and back up the message that fruit and vegetables can be tasty and fun.

Headings: each of the main sections has a heading to attract attention and break up the text.

Bullet points: suggestions for serving are broken up with bullet points making it quick and easy to read.

Columns: these are used to break up the text into manageable chunks; the columns are themselves broken up with pictures.

This leaflet was produced by the charity Help The Aged to advertise a service called SeniorLink.

You need never feel alone

peace of mind at the touch of a button

Help the Aged
SeniorLink
Immediate Response Service

At Help the Aged, we care about older people. We believe that you should always feel safe and secure in your own home, particularly if you choose to live on your own. That's why we have developed SeniorLink - an immediate response service linking you to the people who care about you. And it is available to everyone.

SeniorLink gives you greater independence, security and confidence, whilst providing your family and friends with peace of mind, safe in the knowledge that we'll always be there for you.

Using your telephone line, the SeniorLink system allows you to contact us instantly.

At the touch of a button - either on your SeniorLink unit or on your personal pendant, you will immediately be connected to our round-the-clock Response Centre, from anywhere in your home or garden. Our team of highly skilled staff will quickly respond to your need.

Whether you are anxious and want reassurance, in need of emergency assistance, or you simply want a friendly chat - we are ready to take your call, anytime, day or night.

To make it easier for you to join SeniorLink, we offer a range of flexible, affordable payment options which allow you to choose a method that's right for you.

With SeniorLink, you can live in the comfort of your own home safe in the knowledge that our service offers you:

- Immediate response at the touch of a button
- Contact 24 hours a day, 365 days a year
- Professional help from our highly trained team
- More than just an emergency contact - a friend to turn to anytime
- Greater independence, security and confidence
- Peace of mind for you, your family and friends.

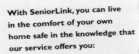
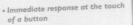

TEL. 01483 729678
FOR ALL ENQUIRIES

Claire Rayner sums it up:
"In a very practical and caring way SeniorLink removes a big worry. It supports our independence and the wish to live in our own home."

<u>Read</u> the text   <u>Annotate</u> the text   <u>Answer</u> the questions

Basic questions

Who is it aimed at?

Why has it been written?

What is the main idea/ message in the text?

How is that message put across?

SATS QUESTIONS

1. Find and copy an example of a fact and an opinion used in this text and explain how each is effective.

Fact:
Explanation:

Opinion:
Explanation: (4 marks)

2. Which personal pronouns are most often used and what effect does this have?

Personal pronouns:

Explanation: (2 marks)

3. Write about the way in which layout and presentational devices have been used to persuade the reader to subscribe to the SeniorLink scheme. Write your answer on a separate sheet.

Write about:
• **The use of pictures**
• **Font size and style**
• **General organisation**   (6 marks)

FEATURES OF IMAGINATIVE WRITING

Creating a good piece of imaginative writing is similar to following a recipe. There are some basic ingredients that you need to include. They are:

- plot/story-line
- characterisation
- relationships
- setting
- descriptive language
- dialogue.

These are the same elements that were discussed in Reading Fiction Texts. Go back to that chapter for more information.

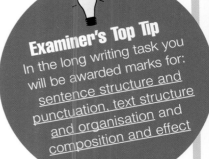

WRITING TO IMAGINE, EXPLORE, ENTERTAIN

In your SAT exams you will have to complete two writing tasks – a long task worth 30 marks and a short task worth 20 marks. If this writing triplet is tested, it is more likely to be in the long writing task.

TO ACHIEVE LEVEL 5 YOU NEED TO:

- think of an <u>interesting</u> <u>story-line</u>
- <u>organise</u> <u>your</u> <u>writing</u> to hold interest
- make use of <u>interesting</u> <u>words</u> <u>and</u> <u>phrases</u>
- include some <u>conversation</u>.

TO MOVE FROM LEVEL 5 TO LEVELS 6 AND 7 YOU ALSO NEED TO:

- create <u>believable</u> <u>characters</u>
- create <u>atmosphere</u> – tension and suspense etc.
- use <u>language</u> for particular effects
- use <u>structure</u> to create effects.

BEFORE YOU BEGIN – IMAGINATIVE WRITING

Before you begin to write you will need to <u>plan</u> and make some decisions.

DECIDE:
- what kind of story you want to write
- a basic <u>plot</u> <u>outline</u>
- third- or first-person <u>narrative</u>
- who your <u>main</u> <u>characters</u> are
- where the story is <u>set</u>.

PLAN:
- the content of the <u>beginning</u>, <u>middle</u> and <u>end</u> of your story (see <u>structure</u> pages 50–51)
- character detail
- some <u>descriptive</u> detail.

> **Examiner's Top Tip**
> In the <u>National</u> <u>Curriculum</u>, writing at <u>level 5</u> is described as: '<u>varied</u> and <u>interesting</u> … vocabulary choices are <u>imaginative</u>.'

MAKING YOUR WRITING MORE INTERESTING – EXTENDING VOCABULARY

THAT'S NICE

- In order to achieve <u>Level 5</u> you have to <u>make</u> <u>use</u> <u>of</u> <u>interesting</u> <u>words</u> <u>and</u> <u>phrases</u>. Think about how you can <u>extend</u> <u>your</u> <u>vocabulary</u> by replacing everyday words with something a little more imaginative.
- Instead of <u>nice</u> how about:

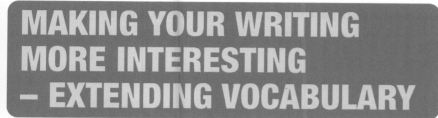

great   amazing   breath taking   beautiful   attractive

superb   lovely   fine   excellent   magnificent

THAT'S REALLY NICE…

Some words are more powerful than others. Your choice of vocabulary should also take account of how strong a word is. What order would you put these words and phrases in?

really nice	warm
absolutely fantastic	hot
quite good	scorched
satisfactory	boiling
appalling	tepid
very entertaining	balmy
reasonably satisfied	fiery

Have a go…

Think of <u>five</u> alternatives for each of the following words. Try to put them in order according to how powerful each word is.

<u>scared</u>
<u>excited</u>
<u>run</u>
<u>fall</u>
<u>angry</u>
<u>cold</u>

> **Examiner's Top Tip**
> When you read fiction at home and at school, try to identify the techniques used by the author and think about how you could use similar devices in your own writing.

WRITING TO IMAGINE, EXPLORE, ENTERTAIN – CHARACTERS AND ATMOSPHERE

> *To keep your writing interesting, you need to think beyond an exciting story-line. You must also create <u>believable</u> <u>characters</u> and <u>the</u> <u>right</u> <u>atmosphere</u>.*

CREATING ATMOSPHERE

The main elements used to create atmosphere are:
- the setting
- the way a character behaves
- use of language devices
- sentence structure
- vocabulary choices.

If you wanted to create a frightening atmosphere, you might include some of the following ideas:

<u>Setting</u>: city at night, forest, beach during winter, castle or unoccupied building

<u>Character</u> <u>behaviour</u>: nervous, jumpy

<u>Language</u> <u>devices</u>: shadows danced like demented spirits

<u>Sentence</u> <u>structure</u>: short sentences and repetition

<u>Vocabulary</u>: isolated, deserted, gloomy, dank, murky

BELIEVABLE CHARACTERS

If the characters in your stories are to be convincing you need to <u>know</u> <u>them</u> before you start writing. Making a character fact file is an effective way to do this.

HAVE A GO NOW...

Name: Leisure/hobbies:

Age: Ambition:

Occupation: Fears:

Appearance: Family:

Personality: Past/secret:

CONVINCING DIALOGUE

Examiner's Top Tip
When you include dialogue in your writing, make sure you use correct speech punctuation. See page 89 for the rules.

Dialogue is another word for speech or conversation. Most fiction contains dialogue because it allows the main characters to communicate with each other. Dialogue is important for the following reasons:

- It helps to bring the characters to life.
- It reveals new information about the character speaking or the character being spoken about.
- It adds variety to the story.

It is important to think about how characters say things as well as what they say.

The exclamation marks show that Billy is in pain or discomfort.

Notice that the conversation is written as these people would really speak. 'Gi'o'er' is how Billy would say 'Give over'. Billy doesn't speak in Standard English – this style of writing indicates Billy's dialect and accent.

Mr Sugden's final comment shows that he thinks Billy is a liar.

Re-read this conversation from *A Kestrel for a Knave*. You read a longer extract in the Fiction Test (pages 16–17). Think about what we learn about the characters from this dialogue.

The conversation isn't always written in complete sentences because we don't always speak in complete sentences.

> 'Got a sweat on Casper?'
> 'Let me out, Sir. Let me come.'
> 'I thought you'd like a cooler after your exertions in goal.'
> 'I'm frozen!'
> 'Really?'
> 'Gi'o'er, Sir! It's not right!'
> 'And was it right when you let that last goal in?'
> 'I couldn't help it!'
> 'Rubbish, lad.'

The whole conversation shows that Mr Sugden is more powerful than Billy.

I SAID, HE SAID, SHE SAID...

- Notice that the example above doesn't use any speech descriptors (verbs) – he said, Billy shouted.
- When you use dialogue in a story think about all the different ways there are to describe how somebody says something. Using a variety of speech descriptors gives the reader more information about what a character is like.
- Here are some words you could use to replace said:

asked   giggled

replied   gasped   shrieked

squeaked   laughed   screamed   exclaimed   snapped

stammered   urged   answered   shouted   whispered

Have a go...   Decide on a speech descriptor for each line in the conversation above. Choose from the list or use your own ideas.

WRITING TO IMAGINE, EXPLORE, ENTERTAIN – LANGUAGE AND STRUCTURE

Effective use of language and control of the structure of your writing will help you to score high marks in all strands of the long writing task.

USING LANGUAGE

ADJECTIVES AND ADVERBS
Make use of descriptive words to make your writing interesting. For example, <u>He sat down</u> at <u>the table</u>. (simple sentence)
<u>Wearily</u>, <u>he sat down</u> at the <u>old</u>, <u>worn table</u>.

adverb   noun phrase using adjectives

Examiner's Top Tip
Time spent planning is time well spent. In the long writing task, you are given 15 minutes to plan. Think about what you are going to write and how you are going to sustain your narrative.

COLOURS
Using colour in your descriptions can make them more interesting, especially if you try to be more adventurous than using yellow, red, blue etc. Here is a list of colours used by Susan Hill in the extract you read earlier: <u>ragged black wings; butter-coloured corn stalks; its mouth was scarlet; the tip of its black wing</u>.

IMAGERY
Use <u>similes</u>, <u>metaphors</u> and <u>personification</u> in your writing.

SENSES
Include images or descriptions that will appeal to the five senses. For example, <u>rubbing the damp mess of tears and sweat off his face with one hand</u>. (*I'm the King of the Castle* by Susan Hill)

SENTENCE STRUCTURE
- Try to vary the length and construction of your sentences. This will make your writing more interesting. It will also allow you to use <u>sentence</u> <u>structure</u> for effect. If you have been writing fairly <u>complex</u> <u>sentences</u>, then a sudden change to <u>short</u>, <u>simple</u> <u>sentences</u> could show sudden fear.
- Here is another extract from Susan Hill's writing: <u>Sweat</u> <u>was</u> <u>running</u> <u>down</u> <u>his</u> <u>forehead</u> <u>and</u> <u>into</u> <u>his</u> <u>eyes</u>. <u>He</u> <u>looked</u> <u>up</u>. <u>The</u> <u>crow</u> <u>kept</u> <u>on</u> <u>coming</u>. <u>He</u> <u>ran</u>.
- She could have written: <u>He</u> <u>looked</u> <u>up</u> <u>and</u> <u>saw</u> <u>that</u> <u>the</u> <u>crow</u> <u>kept</u> <u>on</u> <u>coming</u> <u>so</u> <u>he</u> <u>ran</u>. All the dramatic tension is lost in this version.

STRUCTURE

Your writing needs clearly defined structure. This will usually take the form of three definite stages: <u>the</u> <u>beginning</u>, the <u>middle</u> <u>and</u> <u>the</u> <u>ending</u>.

THE BEGINNING

- In the opening section of a piece of imaginative writing, you need to introduce the <u>characters</u> and the <u>setting</u>, and begin to <u>develop</u> <u>the</u> <u>main</u> <u>plot</u> <u>strands</u>.
- It is important to <u>create</u> <u>an</u> <u>interesting</u> <u>opening</u>, as you need to capture the attention of your reader.
- Do not give your reader too much detail. Keep them guessing so that they will want to read on. <u>Never</u> <u>launch</u> <u>straight</u> <u>into</u> 'telling <u>a</u> <u>story</u>'.
- Begin with an interesting <u>description</u> <u>of</u> <u>a</u> <u>character</u> <u>or</u> <u>the</u> <u>setting</u>.
- If you are writing in <u>first-person</u> <u>narrative</u>, you could begin with an intriguing statement from your main character.

THE MIDDLE

- In the central section of your writing you need to <u>develop</u> <u>plot</u>, <u>characterisation</u> and <u>relationships</u>. Development is essential if you are to hold the interest of the reader.
- If you made a <u>character</u> <u>fact</u> <u>file</u> as preparation, make sure you introduce some details from it. Refer back to your character plans to make sure they react to events in the way their personality suggests.
- Think about how you can use <u>language</u> <u>and</u> <u>structure</u> to make your writing interesting and lively.

THE ENDING

In the final section of your writing, you must begin to tie up loose ends. You have three main options for finishing your writing:

- <u>Cliffhanger</u>: the story ends without <u>conclusion</u> <u>or</u> <u>resolution</u>. This keeps the reader guessing as to what will happen next. However, you need to <u>leave</u> <u>some</u> <u>clues</u> and have some ideas yourself for what will happen next. You should plan to finish in this way rather than realising you have run out of time. An unfinished ending and a cliffhanger ending are two completely different things!
- <u>Twist</u> <u>in</u> <u>the</u> <u>tale</u>: a completely unexpected twist in the plot right at the end. This is an exciting way to end a story but it is also more difficult to manage. Again, it is important to plan for this kind of ending.
- <u>Resolution</u>: all the loose ends are tied up and the <u>ending</u> <u>is</u> <u>complete</u> <u>and</u> <u>definite</u>. This would often be a happy ending but it doesn't have to be.

<u>Try to</u> <u>avoid</u> <u>clichéd</u> <u>endings</u>. You could really ruin a good story for want of an original conclusion. For example, avoid: 'Then I woke up. It had all been a dream!'

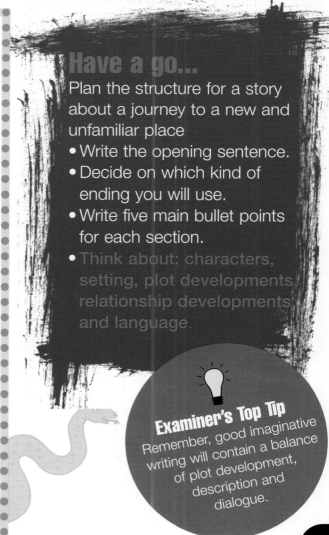

Have a go...

Plan the structure for a story about a journey to a new and unfamiliar place
- Write the opening sentence.
- Decide on which kind of ending you will use.
- Write five main bullet points for each section.
- Think about: characters, setting, plot developments, relationship developments and language.

Examiner's Top Tip
Remember, good imaginative writing will contain a balance of plot development, description and dialogue.

GOOD NON-FICTION

To produce a good piece of **non-fiction** writing you need to have a clear sense of purpose. You need to know what you are trying to achieve as an end result. Usually it will be one of the following:

- **communicate information or ideas**
- **persuade people to buy something, take part in something or change their opinion about something**
- **express your own opinion.**

In every situation you will be targeting a specific **audience**.
You need to keep that at the front of your mind when you write. Hopefully, this will help you to keep your writing direct and focused.

Examiner's Top Tip
In the short writing task you will be awarded marks for: sentence structure, punctuation and text organisation; composition and effect and spelling.

WRITING TO INFORM AND EXPLAIN

In the long and short **writing tasks** in the National Tests you may be required to write in one of the following styles.
Writing to:

- **inform, explain, describe**
- **persuade, argue, advise**
- **review, analyse, comment**

You may have to write in one or more of the following forms:

letter	speech
leaflet	review
newspaper or magazine article	essay

Basic questions

In the Reading Non-fiction and Media sections of this book, you were advised to ask yourself four basic questions after reading a text. When you write a non-fiction piece, you should be able to apply those same questions to your own work. If the answers are clear then you have done a good job. Those questions are:

WHO is it aimed at?

WHY has it been written?

WHAT is the main idea/ message in the text?

HOW is that message put across?

TO ACHIEVE LEVEL 5 YOU NEED TO:

- <u>organise</u> your ideas in a clear way
- <u>interest</u> and <u>persuade</u> your reader
- make use of a <u>formal style</u> and <u>Standard English</u> where appropriate
- <u>support</u> your <u>ideas</u> with <u>evidence</u>, <u>examples</u> and <u>quotations</u>
- begin to <u>develop</u> some of your ideas fully.

TO MOVE FROM LEVEL 5 TO LEVELS 6 AND 7 YOU ALSO NEED TO:

- make use of particular <u>language devices</u> for effect
- use <u>structure</u> to create effects
- show an <u>awareness</u> of the <u>audience and purpose</u> you are writing for.

WRITING TO INFORM

Conventions of information text:
- uses <u>sub-headings</u>
- text is written in the <u>present</u> <u>tense</u>
- uses <u>third</u> <u>person</u>
- the <u>length</u> <u>of</u> <u>sentences</u> is decided by the need for clarity – mostly <u>simple</u> and <u>compound</u> <u>sentences</u>
- <u>examples</u>, diagrams and illustrations <u>back</u> <u>up</u> <u>the</u> <u>information</u> in the text.

Examiner's Top Tip
Explanation sometimes contains elements of other non-fiction styles: <u>information</u> and <u>persuasion</u>.

VISUAL VARIETY

Remember that a successful information text needs to hold the reader's attention. Think about the way you can improve the visual impact of your information text:
- <u>bullet</u> <u>points</u>
- pictures
- <u>headings</u>
- <u>different</u> font sizes and styles
- colour
- <u>tables</u>, <u>charts</u> <u>and</u> <u>graphs</u>
- <u>paragraph</u> <u>length</u>

PLANNING

Decide on the categories of information you are going to provide.

WRITING

Your writing style needs to be clear, factual and formal. As you are required to write in the third person, you should use terms such as: <u>Students</u> <u>study</u> <u>a</u> <u>wide</u> <u>range</u> <u>of</u> <u>subjects</u>.
<u>Don't</u> use <u>we</u> or <u>I</u>: At school <u>we</u> study lots of different subjects.

WRITING TO EXPLAIN

You may be asked to explain:

Why?

A point of view

How?

A decision

A process

Conventions of explanation:
- the opening contains a <u>general</u> <u>statement</u> to introduce the topic
- the development of the explanation draws attention to <u>how</u> something works or <u>why</u> something happens
- there is a <u>summary</u> of what has been explained
- text is written in the <u>present</u> <u>tense</u>
- text uses the <u>passive</u> <u>voice</u> and technical vocabulary, which gives the piece quite a <u>formal</u> <u>style</u>
- uses <u>connectives</u> that indicate <u>cause and effect</u>
- uses <u>connectives</u> that indicate <u>sequence</u>.

Use the following connectives in your own writing.

CAUSE AND EFFECT

| because | so | due to |
| therefore | as a result of | |

SEQUENCE

| then | next |
| finally | gradually |

WRITING TO DESCRIBE

You could be asked to write a _description_ of:
- *a PERSON*
- *a PLACE*
- *or a PARTICULAR MEMORY*

You will also use writing to describe techniques in _writing to imagine_, _explore and entertain_.
It is often a good idea to note down _adjectives_, _images_ and _particular details_ you want to include in your writing before you decide on the structure of your writing.

DESCRIBING PEOPLE

If you are asked to describe a person in detail, you need to think about lots of different aspects of that person, not just what they looked like.

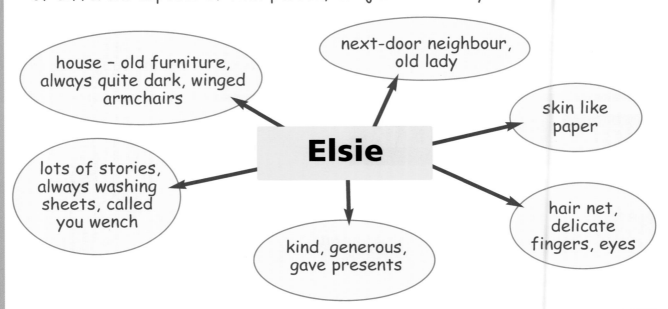

next-door neighbour, old lady

house – old furniture, always quite dark, winged armchairs

skin like paper

Elsie

lots of stories, always washing sheets, called you wench

hair net, delicate fingers, eyes

kind, generous, gave presents

Examiner's Top Tip
Use your planning as a starting point. You are bound to develop and change your ideas and images as you get into your writing. Don't feel bound to use the exact words and phrases you came up with in your planning.

A person I remember clearly from my childhood is my next-door neighbour, Elsie. She was the oldest person I knew. Her skin was like crinkly brown paper and her eyes watered when she laughed. She had delicate, mottled hands and her wedding ring was loose on her finger. She was generous and kind. Whenever we visited we had jelly sweets or jaffa cakes. She called me 'wench' or 'ducks'. She always seemed to be washing sheets and took great pride in always being first out to hang her washing on the line.

DESCRIBING MEMORIES

The spider diagram below is planning to answer the following question:

Describe a journey you remember well.

Examiner's Top Tip
It is perfectly acceptable to make up some or all of the details in a piece of descriptive writing. The quality of your writing is being tested, not the accuracy of your memory.

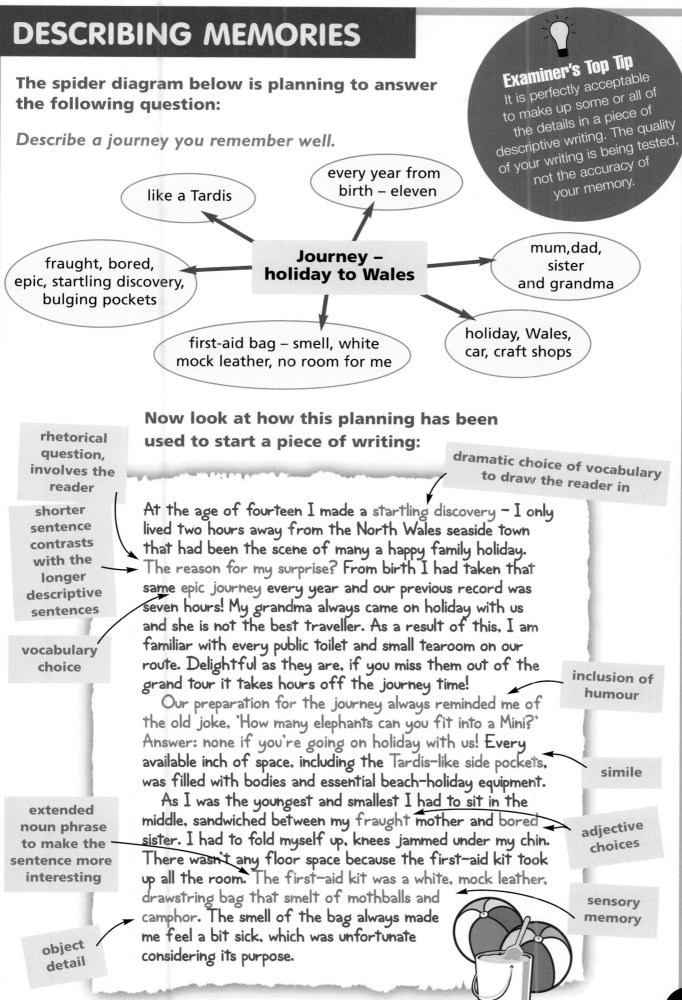

like a Tardis

every year from birth – eleven

fraught, bored, epic, startling discovery, bulging pockets

Journey – holiday to Wales

mum, dad, sister and grandma

first-aid bag – smell, white mock leather, no room for me

holiday, Wales, car, craft shops

Now look at how this planning has been used to start a piece of writing:

rhetorical question, involves the reader

shorter sentence contrasts with the longer descriptive sentences

vocabulary choice

dramatic choice of vocabulary to draw the reader in

At the age of fourteen I made a startling discovery – I only lived two hours away from the North Wales seaside town that had been the scene of many a happy family holiday. The reason for my surprise? From birth I had taken that same epic journey every year and our previous record was seven hours! My grandma always came on holiday with us and she is not the best traveller. As a result of this, I am familiar with every public toilet and small tearoom on our route. Delightful as they are, if you miss them out of the grand tour it takes hours off the journey time!

Our preparation for the journey always reminded me of the old joke, 'How many elephants can you fit into a Mini?' Answer: none if you're going on holiday with us! Every available inch of space, including the Tardis-like side pockets, was filled with bodies and essential beach-holiday equipment.

As I was the youngest and smallest I had to sit in the middle, sandwiched between my fraught mother and bored sister. I had to fold myself up, knees jammed under my chin. There wasn't any floor space because the first-aid kit took up all the room. The first-aid kit was a white, mock leather, drawstring bag that smelt of mothballs and camphor. The smell of the bag always made me feel a bit sick, which was unfortunate considering its purpose.

inclusion of humour

simile

adjective choices

extended noun phrase to make the sentence more interesting

sensory memory

object detail

WRITING TO PERSUADE

Most persuasive texts use some or all of the following devices:
emotive language, repetition, rhetorical questions, presenting opinion as fact, counter-argument, evidence

EMOTIVE LANGUAGE is the use of words and phrases that evoke an emotional response. You will find lots of emotive language in advertisements and charity appeals. Which is more persuasive?

- Please give £10 to help this child.
- Just £10 will save David from torment and starvation. Please act now to give him a better, brighter future.

When you are choosing vocabulary for your persuasive writing, remember that some words have more emotive power then others. Think about the emotive power of these words:

DIED   KILLED   EXECUTED   SLAUGHTERED   GROUP   CROWD   GANG   MOB

REPETITION helps to reinforce the main points of your text and build up a pattern and a rhythm in your writing. Repetition is particularly useful if you are writing a talk or speech. It will help your audience to remember your main points. Think about the different kinds of repetition you could use.

- You might repeat an emotive phrase at the end of each paragraph.
- You might repeatedly emphasise a good or bad feature of an object, person or situation you are writing about.
- You might try to use some repetitive sentence structures. Look at the final sentence from the argument text below and think about the way repetition has been used:
  It is uncomfortable; it is unfashionable; it is impractical and it has to go!

RHETORICAL QUESTIONS do not expect or require an answer. They are used to achieve strong emphasis. The writer assumes that the answer to the question is obvious. The question 'How old are you?' clearly requires an answer, whereas 'Makes you think, doesn't it?' is rhetorical and assumes that the answer will be yes.

Example Introduction

In an era of continual educational change, schools are expected to keep up to date with the latest technologies and teaching styles to provide the very best educational experience for their students. Why then do most schools insist on continuing the outdated and constraining institution of school uniform? It is uncomfortable; it is unfashionable; it is impractical and it has to go!

ARGUMENT

Argument is a form of persuasion. If you have a verbal argument with somebody, it is because you disagree with their opinion. To win an argument you must persuade your opponent that your point of view is correct

A one-sided essay expresses your own opinions about an issue. You may also be asked to write a one-sided argument in the form of a letter or speech. It should be structured as follows:

1. Introduction explaining the issue and giving your opinion.

2. A series of paragraphs to express the main points of your argument. You should include evidence to support your ideas. It is essential that you have a clear argument running through your essay. You should organise your points so that one builds on the next. Make sure you order your points to have the most impact.

3. Conclusion summing up your main points and restating your opinion.

DISCURSIVE ESSAY

A discursive or balanced essay considers two sides of an issue or argument. It should be structured as follows:

1. <u>Introduction</u> explaining the issue.

2. An <u>organised</u> <u>series</u> <u>of</u> <u>paragraphs</u> with points in favour of the issue.

3. An <u>organised</u> <u>series</u> <u>of</u> <u>paragraphs</u> with points against the issue.

4. <u>Conclusion</u> summing up the points for and against and giving your own opinion.

LINKING POINTS IN YOUR ARGUMENT

Use the following connectives to link your ideas in persuasion and argument texts:

furthermore	on the other hand	despite the fact that
however	nevertheless	not only
of course	in my opinion	

Examiner's Top Tip
<u>Discursive argument</u> and <u>advice</u> sometimes use <u>rhetorical questions</u> to introduce new topics or ideas.

WRITING TO PERSUADE, ARGUE, ADVISE

SHOULDA, WOULDA, COULDA – WRITING TO ADVISE

Lots of advice texts contain the <u>modal verbs</u> should, would and could. Look at these examples from advice for looking after a new pet:

- You <u>should</u> take your dog for a walk at least once a day.
- You <u>could</u> try basic obedience training once your puppy is old enough.
- I <u>would</u> suggest a regular check up with vet.

Other conventions of advice:
- uses the <u>imperative</u>
- text is written in the <u>second person</u>
- makes <u>suggestions</u>
- can use <u>anecdote</u>/examples
- sentences tend to be simpler to get information across
- sometimes uses <u>rhetorical questions</u> to introduce ideas.

Have a go...
Plan a persuasive letter or leaflet about animal cruelty. Include emotive language, rhetorical questions, repetition and evidence to support your ideas.

WRITING TO REVIEW, ANALYSE, COMMENT

You may be required to write in this form in either the long writing task or the short writing task in your SAT exams. You will also use analysis and comment skills in the Reading Paper and the reading section of the Shakespeare Paper.

WRITING TO REVIEW

When you write a review of something, you are giving your own opinion. This could be completely different from somebody else's opinion on the same topic. You might be asked to write a review about:

- a book
- a film
- a television programme
- an exhibition.

WHAT TO INCLUDE

Although a review is made up largely of your opinion, you will probably need to provide the reader with some facts and information.

- The title and author/director etc.
- A summary of the story.
- Information about the exhibition.
- Where you can buy the book or see the film/exhibition.

The audience of a written review will usually be people who want to know if they would enjoy the book, film or exhibition. You should include your opinions on:

- its strengths
- its weaknesses
- its suitability for a particular audience.

WRITING TO ANALYSE AND COMMENT

This is probably the most formal style of writing you will be required to use in your exams.

WRITING STYLE

- Text is written in the third person.
- Opinions are expressed in a detached way – avoid phrases such as 'I think that...'
- Opinions are supported by textual evidence.
- Avoid non-standard forms and colloquial expression.

Examiner's Top Tip
Use Standard English when you write to analyse or comment.

STRUCTURE

An analytical essay should follow a set pattern:

- <u>Introduction</u> should refer to key words in the question, capture the attention of the reader and demonstrate an understanding of the question.
- A <u>series</u> <u>of</u> <u>paragraphs</u> exploring different aspects of the question. Paragraphs should be linked and main points should be supported with quotation.
- <u>Conclusion</u> should refer back to the main points of your analysis and give your personal response to the question.

PARAGRAPH STRUCTURE

A useful way to structure your analysis in each paragraph is:

- make a <u>statement</u> or comment
- use quotation or textual evidence to <u>back</u> <u>up</u> your statement
- <u>explain</u> your comment with reference to the evidence you have cited.

This is often referred to as the <u>PEE</u> <u>structure</u> – <u>Point</u>, <u>Evidence</u>, <u>Explanation</u> or <u>PEC</u> – <u>Point</u>, <u>Evidence</u>, <u>Comment</u>.

Examiner's Top Tip
When writing <u>analysis</u> and <u>comment</u>, remember to <u>flex your PECs!</u>

SOME USEFUL PHRASES...

Use these phrases to help you comment on the effects created by literature and non-fiction texts:

> this suggests that...
>
> the author conveys a sense of ... by ...
>
> this is effective because...
>
> this evokes a feeling of...
>
> he creates tension by...
>
> the writer aims to persuade...

TRY TO AVOID...

> I know this because...
>
> it says...
>
> the writer quotes...
>
> this quotation shows that...

Examiner's Top Tip
When you are writing to <u>review</u>, keep your <u>audience</u> in mind. Make sure your language is suitable for the audience you have been asked to write for.

WRITING MEDIA TEXTS

The main media text types you could be asked to write are:

- leaflets
- advertisements
- magazine/newspaper articles

A good way to learn how to write in this style is to study examples of the style. Re-read the media sections of this book. The glossary on pages 38–39 explains the technical terms.

LEAFLETS

- Leaflets are usually free and are often handed out or posted through your door at home. For this reason it is important to make an <u>immediate</u> <u>visual</u> <u>impact</u> through the use of <u>pictures</u> or bold, eye-catching <u>headings</u>.
- <u>Information</u>, <u>advice</u> or <u>opinion</u> needs to be presented in a clear and concise way.
- Information in leaflets needs to appear to be directed at the individual reader. For this reason you should use <u>personal</u> <u>pronouns</u>.

LAYOUT AND PRESENTATION
The main devices you would use in a leaflet are:

- bullet points
- columns
- pictures
- short paragraphs
- headings

Have a go...
Write five bullet points about the disadvantages of smoking, aimed at teenagers.

1. ....
2. ....
3. ....
4. ....
5. ....

Think of two presentational devices you might use in a leaflet to persuade teenagers to give up smoking.

1. ....
2. ....

Think of two pictures you could use in the same leaflet.

1. ....
2. ....

Examiner's Top Tip
If you want to include pictures in a leaflet simply draw a box and write what the picture would be.

ADVERTISEMENTS

As advertising relies so heavily on pictures, it is unlikely that you would be required to write an advertisement in your exam.

Some leaflets have an <u>advertising function</u> as well as offering <u>advice</u> or <u>information</u>.

Advertising language is very <u>persuasive</u>. If you were asked to design an advert you should think about the following:

- emotive and persuasive language
- devices such as alliteration, repetition, puns and questions
- how to present opinions in a factual way.

LAYOUT AND PRESENTATION

The main devices you would use are:
- pictures
- different font styles and sizes.

The main points to remember when you are writing a media text are:
- the purpose is usually to <u>persuade</u> although it could also be to <u>advise</u> or to <u>inform</u>
- clever <u>use</u> of <u>language</u> is essential
- you want people to <u>remember</u> your main <u>message</u>
- you need to be <u>concise</u> and <u>precise</u>
- <u>layout</u> and <u>presentational</u> <u>devices</u> are essential.

Have a go...
- Think of a new product name and slogan for a box of chocolates.
- Write appealing descriptions of the following chocolates from your new range.

    Strawberry cream
    Caramel
    Dark chocolate and hazelnut
    Orange fondant

....
....
....
....
....
....
....
....
....

Have a go...
- Write a headline and topic sentence about a lottery winner for a local newspaper.
- Think of two people you would interview for your article.
- Think of a photograph you would want for the story and write a caption to go with it.

....
....
....
....
....
....
....
....

MAGAZINES/NEWSPAPERS

- News articles report something that has already happened so you must always write in the <u>past</u> <u>tense</u>.
- News articles usually report the most dramatic part of an event first and then retell the rest of the story in chronological order.
- News articles are written in <u>Standard</u> <u>English</u>. The only exception to this is direct quotation, which will be written exactly as the person said it.

LAYOUT AND PRESENTATION

The main devices you would use are:
- pictures
- columns
- short paragraphs
- headlines.

Examiner's Top Tip
Remember: it is the quality of your writing that is being tested. Don't spend all your time colouring in.

61

WRITING LETTERS, ESSAYS AND SPEECHES

WRITING A FORMAL LETTER

There are many reasons why you may need to write a formal letter. For example: to apply for a job; to complain to a company; to apply for a membership; to book a service or to request permission.

There are a lot of <u>conventions</u> to follow when you are writing a formal letter.

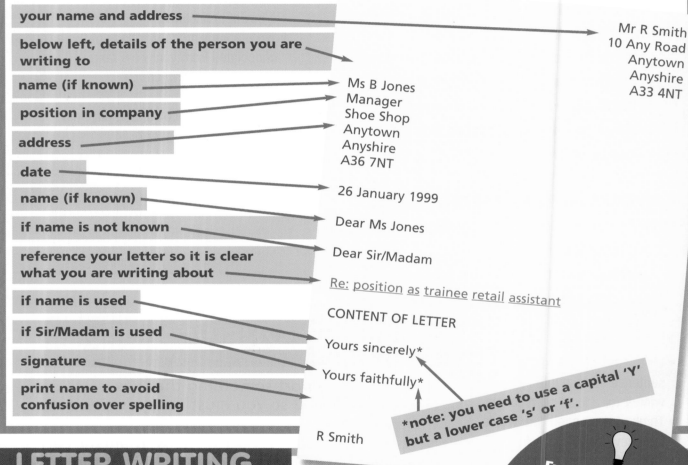

your name and address

Mr R Smith
10 Any Road
Anytown
Anyshire
A33 4NT

below left, details of the person you are writing to

name (if known)

Ms B Jones

position in company

Manager
Shoe Shop

address

Anytown
Anyshire
A36 7NT

date

26 January 1999

name (if known)

Dear Ms Jones

if name is not known

Dear Sir/Madam

reference your letter so it is clear what you are writing about

<u>Re: position as trainee retail assistant</u>

if name is used

CONTENT OF LETTER

if Sir/Madam is used

Yours sincerely*

signature

Yours faithfully*

print name to avoid confusion over spelling

*note: you need to use a capital 'Y' but a lower case 's' or 'f'.

R Smith

LETTER WRITING DOS AND DON'TS

On many occasions when you write a formal letter, you will be writing to somebody that you have never met before. Remember the following points:

- <u>Do</u> use <u>Standard English</u>.
- <u>Don't</u> use <u>slang</u> or conversational language.
- Try not to be either aggressive or over-familiar in your tone.
- Get to your point quickly and stick to your point.

In an exam you have plenty of time to <u>plan</u> the content, structure and accuracy of your letter. Think about the topics that you want to cover and decide on the best order to write about them so your writing flows.

Examiner's Top Tip
If the exam task instructs you to write to a friend then the layout of your letter can be more informal. You may also use some conversational language and/or slang but it would be advisable to write most of the letter in <u>Standard English</u>.

STANDARD ENGLISH

Formal letters, essays and speeches all require a <u>formal</u> style and <u>Standard English</u>. The following non-standard forms should be avoided.

USING ADJECTIVES AS ADVERBS

She won <u>easy</u>. ✗

She won <u>easily</u>. ✔

MIXING <u>SINGULAR</u> AND <u>PLURAL</u> IN SUBJECT/VERB AGREEMENT

He <u>were</u> frightened. ✗

He <u>was</u> frightened. ✔

We <u>was</u> bad. ✗

We <u>were</u> bad. ✔

USING '<u>THEM</u>' AS A <u>DETERMINER</u>

I bought <u>them</u> oranges. ✗

I bought <u>those</u> oranges. ✔

USING '<u>WHAT</u>' AS A <u>RELATIVE</u> PRONOUN

Have you seen the book <u>what</u> I bought? ✗

Have you seen the book <u>that</u> I bought? ✔

WRITING ESSAYS

In your SAT exams you may be required to write a persuasive essay, a discursive essay or a literary criticism essay that offers analysis and comment on the Shakespeare scenes you have studied.

All essays follow these conventions:
*   uses <u>formal language/Standard English</u>
*   usually written in the <u>third person</u>
*   use of <u>evidence</u>, <u>quotation</u> and/or <u>textual reference</u> to support opinion
*   follows a <u>structure</u> – introduction, series of linked paragraphs developing a line of argument, conclusion

You will find further information about writing essays on <u>pages 56-59</u>.

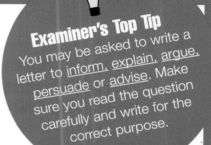

Examiner's Top Tip
You may be asked to write a letter to <u>inform</u>, <u>explain</u>, <u>argue</u>, <u>persuade</u> or <u>advise</u>. Make sure you read the question carefully and write for the correct purpose.

WRITING SPEECHES

The most important thing to remember about a speech is that your intended audience will be listening to rather than reading what you have written.

Remember this at the planning stage and think about how you can help an audience to follow your line of argument or explanation.

Here are some important devices that make a speech effective:
*   <u>Topic sentences</u> at the beginning of each paragraph will help your audience to understand the key points and to recognise what they should be listening out for.
*   <u>Varied sentence structure</u> and length will allow you to control the pace and rhythms of your speech. This will keep an audience interested.
*   <u>Repetition</u> will help the listener to remember your key points.
*   <u>Rhetorical devices</u>, such as <u>rhetorical questions</u> and listing in groups of three, will also focus your listener on key points.
*   A <u>closing statement</u> that summarises your argument and restates your main point will make sure the listener goes away in no doubt about the opinion you wanted to express.

WRITING TEST

You have 45 minutes to complete this task. You should spend 10–15 minutes planning your writing.

This task is worth 30 marks. You will be awarded marks for:

- **Sentence structure and punctuation**   **(8 marks)**
- **text structure and organisation**   **(8 marks)**
- **composition and effect**   **(14 marks)**

Writing to imagine, entertain, explore

1. 'It wasn't me!'
   Write about someone wrongly suspected or accused of committing a crime.
   Think about:
   - What they have been accused of
   - How that person would feel

2. Write about being lost or followed in a forest.
   - Try to build up an atmosphere of fear
   - Describe the forest
   - Write in the first or third person

Writing to argue, persuade, advise

3. Imagine you are the director of a new museum.
   Write a letter to headteachers of schools in the area persuading them to bring groups of pupils to the museum
   You could write about:
   - What the museum has to offer
   - Why is it of educational value
   - How to organise a trip there

4. Write a discursive essay about keeping animals in zoos and safari parks.
   Write about:
   - The points for keeping animals in captivity
   - The points against keeping animals in captivity
   - Your own opinion

5. Write an advice leaflet for teenagers preparing for exams. Think carefully about your presentation and layout.
   You should include:
   - Advice and suggestions for revision
   - What to do in the exam
   - Tips for relaxing

WRITING TEST

Writing to inform, explain, describe

1. Relationships can be changed or broken up by many things, for example: a move away, death or an argument.

   Write about a close relationship that comes to an end.
   - Describe the relationship
   - Explain why the relationship ended
   - Try to recreate the emotions involved

2. Describe a place you have enjoyed visiting.
   You could write about:
   - Why you like it
   - Any specific memories of the place
   - Why you would recommend other people to visit this place

Writing to persuade, argue, advise

3. Imagine you have been given a chance to give a talk to your class. Choose an issue you feel strongly about.

   Write a short talk trying to persuade other people to support your views.

Remember the four basic questions to ask about a non-fiction text:

Who is it aimed at?

Why has it been written?

What is the main idea/ message in the text?

How is that message put across?

SHAKESPEARE

The Shakespeare paper tests your reading and understanding of the two scenes from the Shakespeare play you have studied. There are three plays to choose from and your teacher will make this decision.

The plays are:

- Macbeth, Much Ado About Nothing, Henry V (2005)
- Macbeth, Much Ado About Nothing, Richard III (2006)
- The Tempest, Much Ado About Nothing, Richard III (2007).

To achieve level 5 you need to:

- show an <u>understanding</u> of the <u>plot</u>
- show some <u>understanding</u> of the <u>feelings</u> and <u>behaviour</u> of the <u>characters</u>
- note the <u>effect of particular words</u> and phrases
- show an understanding of <u>how your scenes fit into the play</u>.

To move from level 5 to levels 6 and 7 you also need to:

- <u>support your ideas</u> about characters and relationships with <u>detailed reference to the text</u>
- write in some detail about the <u>effects of language</u>
- show <u>understanding</u> of the more <u>complex feelings</u> of the characters
- show an <u>awareness</u> of how your scenes are affected by <u>events preceding them</u> and how they affect the <u>action that follows</u>.

WHAT YOU WILL STUDY

- There are <u>two scenes</u> to study from each play.
  Although <u>you only need to study two scenes in detail</u>, it will be helpful to have some knowledge of the rest of the play.
- In the exam there will be <u>one question relating to each play</u>. You will be required to write about both of the scenes you have studied. Your teacher will direct you to the correct question.

Examiner's Top Tip
You need to know your specified scenes very well but you do not need to learn quotations. You will be provided with a copy of the scene with your exam paper.

WHAT YOU WILL BE TESTED ON

Your reading is tested in your response to a question about the Shakespeare scenes you have studied. You must write about both scenes in your answer but you are not required to compare the scenes. The quality of your writing is not assessed in this exam.

EMPATHY/WRITING IN ROLE

You will be asked to imagine yourself to be a character in the scene and to write about how you feel about the events of the play you have been involved in. It is essential that you <u>remain in role</u> and refer to the character as 'I' or '<u>me</u>'. For example, '<u>If I want to become king, I must kill Duncan</u>.'
This type of question tests:
* your understanding of character emotions and reactions
* your understanding of plot development
* your ability to sustain writing in role.

LITERARY CRITICISM

You will be asked to write in a more detached way about:

* how characters behave
* how relationships are developed
* how atmosphere is created
* how language is used.

STAGING

You will be asked to write about how a scene should be performed on stage. This will test:
* **your understanding of key relationships**
* **your understanding of how language is used**
* **your understanding of the ways in which characters develop as the play progresses**
* **your ability to see the text as a piece for performance.**

Examiner's Top Tip
If you have studied the whole play by watching a film version, make sure you do not write about events that occur only in the film.

RHYME AND RHYTHM

<u>Blank</u> <u>verse</u>: unrhymed lines of <u>iambic</u> <u>pentameter</u>. Shakespeare wrote his plays in <u>blank</u> <u>verse</u> because it is versatile, it is not restricted by rhyme and it is the closest to the <u>natural</u> <u>rhythms</u> <u>of</u> <u>speech</u>. This makes it easy to create different moods – anger, love, etc.

<u>Iambic</u> <u>pentameter</u>: describes the number of <u>syllables</u> and <u>stresses</u> in a line, which is known as the <u>meter</u>. A foot is a pair of syllables. An iambic foot is an unstressed syllable followed by a stressed syllable. There are <u>five</u> iambic feet in iambic pentameter.

Canterbury:
It <u>must</u> / be <u>so</u>, / for <u>mir</u> / <u>acles</u> / are <u>ceas'd</u>,
And <u>there</u> / fore <u>we</u> / must <u>needs</u> / ad<u>mit</u> / the <u>means</u>,
How <u>things</u> / are <u>per</u> / fec<u>ted</u>./

(Henry V Act 1, Scene 1)*

Examiner's Top Tip
If you are reading Shakespeare aloud try to read to the punctuation. This will help with the sense of what you are reading.

<u>Rhyming</u> <u>couplets</u>: sometimes Shakespeare wrote in different styles for contrast. More <u>formal</u> and <u>traditional</u> characters making important speeches may speak in <u>rhyming</u> <u>couplets</u> (the lines rhyme in pairs). Because of the constraint of finding rhymes there is less movement and freedom in these speeches. This reflects the characters' formality.

Capulet:
At my poor house look to behold this <u>night</u>
Earth-treading stars that make dark heaven <u>light</u>

(Romeo and Juliet)

<u>Prose</u>: the 'low characters', servants for example, speak in prose rather than verse. This reflects that they have less education and their subject matter is often low or coarse.

Trinculo:
I shall laugh myself to death at this puppy headed monster.
A most scurvy monster: I could find in my heart to beat him –

(The Tempest Act 2, Scene 2)*

Porter:
Marry, sir, nose-painting, sleep, and urine.

(Macbeth Act 2, Scene 3, line 27)*

HOW TO READ SHAKESPEARE ALOUD

Shakespeare's language is always much easier to understand when it is read well. Follow these tips.

- <u>Read</u> <u>to</u> the <u>punctuation</u>. If there is no punctuation at the end of a line then read straight through to the next line.
- <u>Don't</u> <u>rush</u>. Speak clearly and think about what you are saying.
- Words ending in 'd or –ed. If a word is spelt '<u>d</u>, e.g. <u>accus'd</u>, you pronounce it as we would say accused. However, if it is spelt accused in the text you pronounce the <u>-ed</u> as a separate syllable – <u>accuse-ed</u>.
- Think about the <u>tone</u> <u>of</u> <u>voice</u> you should use.
- Think about what your character would do when saying the lines.
- <u>Emphasise</u> the words you think are most important. The natural stresses of iambic pentameter should help you to do this.

UNDERSTANDING SHAKESPEARE'S LANGUAGE

The Shakespeare paper is the part of the test that causes most concern amongst students. Again, as with poetry, this is simply because it is less familiar and perhaps seems unconnected to modern-day concerns. However, Shakespeare's plays cover the same themes as any modern piece of writing: <u>love</u>, <u>jealousy</u>, <u>ambition</u>, <u>family</u> <u>conflicts</u>, <u>murder</u> and <u>intrigue</u>. Once the barriers of language have been broken down it is easy to see this.

THEE ... THOU ... WHO?

art	are	thy	your
hadst	had	whence	where
hence	here	wither	where
ill	bad	wouldst	would
o'er	over		
thee	you		
thou	you	(used with someone very close to you or as an insult)
you	you	(a more distant way of speaking to someone)

Examiner's Top Tip
Hearing Shakespeare's language read aloud helps you to understand the meaning. Try to see a live performance or a video version of the play you are studying.

12–16

The phrase '<u>double</u> <u>trust</u>' emphasises that Macbeth would be breaking Duncan's trust twice. He sets out the reasons logically:
- **1a** – he is his <u>kinsman</u> (relative)
- **1b** – he is a trusted subject
- **2** – Duncan is a guest in his house so he should protect him, not plan to kill him. Macbeth presents himself with a well-reasoned argument against the murder plan.

Examiner's Top Tip
If you pick out language devices you must explain how they are used and why they are effective.

16–18

These lines are more <u>emotive</u>. Macbeth reminds himself of all Duncan's qualities. Words like '<u>meek</u>' and '<u>clear</u>' are used to show that Duncan is virtuous and without sin.

18–19

Macbeth imagines that Duncan's virtues will call out like angels, with <u>voices</u> <u>like</u> <u>trumpets</u>. 'Trumpet-tongued' is a <u>Homeric</u> <u>epithet</u>; this is a compound of two words that defines a distinctive quality of a person or thing. In this case it represents a royal fanfare loudly blasting the news of the murder. <u>The</u> <u>fact</u> <u>that</u> <u>the</u> <u>angels</u> <u>are</u> '<u>trumpet-tongued</u>' <u>emphasises</u> <u>the</u> <u>fact</u> <u>that</u> <u>Duncan</u> <u>is</u> <u>without</u> <u>sin</u>.

EXTRACT

He's here in <u>double</u> <u>trust</u>;
First as I am his kinsman and his subject,
Strong both against the deed; then as his host,
Who should against his murderer shut the door,   15
Not <u>bear</u> <u>the</u> <u>knife</u> myself. Besides this Duncan
Hath borne his faculties so <u>meek</u>, hath been
So <u>clear</u> in his great office, that his virtues
Will plead like angels, <u>trumpet-tongued</u> against
The <u>deep</u> <u>damnation</u> of <u>his</u> <u>taking-off</u>   20
And pity, like a <u>naked</u> <u>newborn</u> <u>babe</u>
striding the blast, or heaven's cherubin horsed
Upon the sightless couriers of the air,
Shall blow <u>the</u> <u>horrid</u> <u>deed</u> in every eye,
That tears shall drown the wind. I have no spur   25
To prick the sides of my intent, but only
<u>Vaulting</u> <u>ambition</u> <u>which</u> <u>o'erleaps</u> <u>itself</u>
<u>and</u> <u>falls</u> <u>on</u> <u>th'other</u> –

Macbeth (Act 1, Scene 7, lines 1–28)

In this speech Macbeth lists all the reasons why he should not murder Duncan.

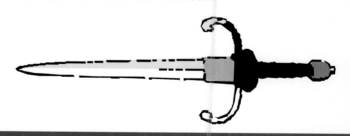

20

Duncan's goodness is contrasted with the '<u>deep</u> <u>damnation</u>' of the act of murder. This is a direct comparison of the spiritual state of the two men, Duncan and Macbeth, his killer. Macbeth realises that he would be damned for eternity for such a sinful act.

SHAKESPEARE'S LANGUAGE – *MACBETH*

The witches have predicted that Macbeth will be king. He and his wife have planned to murder King Duncan. In this soliloquy, Macbeth is having second thoughts.

LANGUAGE DEVICES

- <u>Alliteration</u> is used for emphasis in this speech – '<u>trumpet-tongued</u>', '<u>deep</u> <u>damnation</u>', '<u>naked</u> <u>newborn</u> <u>babe</u>'.
- Throughout this <u>soliloquy</u>, Macbeth uses <u>euphemisms</u> for the murder of Duncan, e.g. '<u>bear</u> <u>the</u> <u>knife</u>', '<u>his</u> <u>taking-off</u>', '<u>horrid</u> <u>deed</u>'. This shows that Macbeth is reluctant to think about the brutality of the act of murder. He is trying to avoid the reality of the situation and cannot face up to the evil nature of the plan that he and his wife have made.
- At the end of this soliloquy, Macbeth has convinced himself not to go ahead with the murder. This part of the soliloquy is in three sections: the reasons why the murder is wrong (lines 12–18); Macbeth's fear of discovery and eternal damnation (lines 18–25) and his want of a 'good' reason to commit the crime (lines 25–28).

21–25

He uses images of innocence and purity – the <u>newborn baby</u> and the <u>cherubin</u> (the highest order of angels) – as the messengers of Duncan's death. They are described as riding the winds (sightless couriers) like horses. <u>Just as a cold wind brings tears to your eyes this news will bring tears to everybody's eyes</u>. He imagines that the winds will be drowned with tears. This emphasises the scale of public mourning for the death of such a king.

25–28

In comparison to all the reasons not to kill Duncan, his only reason to carry out the murder is his <u>ambition</u>. He compares his ambition to <u>a horse that tries to jump too high and falls on the other side of the fence</u>. Macbeth thinks that if he gives in to ambition, he will fail in the end.

Examiner's Top Tip
Remember that religion and the consequences of sin were very important in Shakespeare's time. The power of the language in this soliloquy comes from the religious references.

SHAKESPEARE –
REVISION TECHNIQUES AND TASKS

The following ideas will help you to organise your thoughts about the play you have studied. Once you have completed these tasks, the best way to revise is to answer practice questions. You will find some example questions in the <u>test section</u>.

Make a <u>time line</u> of important events in the play. Leave space to make notes about key scenes and connections between them. For example:

MUCH ADO ABOUT NOTHING

CONNECTIONS	EVENTS
	– Don Pedro and his friends Claudio and Benedick arrive in Messina
	– Beatrice and Benedick renew their war of words
Don John tries to make Claudio jealous later by claiming that Don Pedro woos Hero for himself	– Claudio is in love with Hero, Don Pedro offers to woo Hero on his behalf, Benedick claims he will never fall in love

Make <u>spider diagrams</u> for each of the main characters to trace <u>plot involvement</u>, <u>relationships</u> and <u>personality</u>. For example:

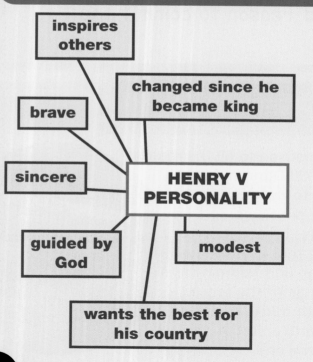

- inspires others
- brave
- changed since he became king
- sincere
- **HENRY V PERSONALITY**
- guided by God
- modest
- wants the best for his country

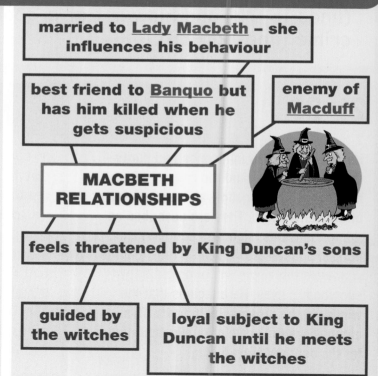

- married to <u>Lady Macbeth</u> – she influences his behaviour
- best friend to <u>Banquo</u> but has him killed when he gets suspicious
- enemy of <u>Macduff</u>
- **MACBETH RELATIONSHIPS**
- feels threatened by King Duncan's sons
- guided by the witches
- loyal subject to King Duncan until he meets the witches

KEY THEMES

Pick out the <u>key</u> <u>themes</u> in your scenes and find <u>quotations</u> that link to this theme in other scenes. If you have your own copy of the play, mark the quotations in your text, using a different colour for each theme. If you don't have your own copy then write out the quotations and colour-code them.

LANGUAGE

Make a close study of the language used by the main characters in your scenes. Think about:
- **how it helps to create an atmosphere**
- **how it helps to show the development of relationships**
- **what it shows us about the personality or intentions of those characters.**

ACTION IN THE REST OF THE PLAY

Make a list or table to show:
- how the action in your scenes is affected by preceding scenes
- how the action in your scenes affects the rest of the play.

Practice questions

Practise questions from the three possible question groups: <u>empathy</u>, <u>literary</u> <u>criticism</u> and <u>staging</u>. You will find some example questions on the following pages.

MUCH ADO ABOUT NOTHING

Leonato:
Confirmed, confirmed, oh that is stronger made,
Which was before barred up with ribs of iron.
Would the two princes lie, and Claudio lie,
Who loved her so, that speaking of her foulness,
Washed it with tears? Hence from her, let her die.

Friar Francis:
Hear me a little, for I have only been
Silent so long, and given way unto
This course of fortune, by noting of the lady.
I have marked
A thousand blushing apparitions,
To start into her face, a thousand innocent shames,
In angel whiteness beat away those blushes,
And in her eye there hath appeared a fire,
To burn the errors that these princes hold
Against her maiden truth: call me a fool,
Trust not my reading, nor my observations,
Which with experimental seal doth warrant
The tenure of my book: trust not my age,
My reverence, calling, nor divinity,
If this sweet lady lie not guiltless here,
Under some biting error.

Much Ado About Nothing (Act 4, Scene 1, lines 143–163)

MACBETH

Macbeth:
That will never be:
Who can impress the forest, bid the tree
Unfix his earth-bound root? Sweet bodements! Good!
Rebellion's head, rise never till the wood
Of Birnam rise, and our high-plac'd Macbeth
Shall live the lease of nature, pay his breath
To time and mortal custom. Yet my heart
Throbs to know one thing: tell me – if your art
Can tell so much – shall Banquo's issue ever
Reign in this kingdom?

(aside) Time, thou anticipat'st my dread exploits;
The flighty purpose never is o'ertook
Unless the deed go with it; from this moment
The very firstlings of my heart shall be
The firstlings of my hand. And even now,
To crown my thoughts with acts, be it thought and done:
The castle of Macduff I will surprise;
Seize upon Fife; give to the edge of the sword
His wife, his babes, and all unfortunate souls
That trace him in his line. No boasting like a fool;
This deed I'll do before this purpose cool:

Macbeth (Act 4, Scene 1, lines 94–103 and 144–154)

SHAKESPEARE LANGUAGE STUDY – *MACBETH, MUCH ADO ABOUT NOTHING* AND *RICHARD III*

Make a close study of the language in the extract from your play. Important <u>words</u>, <u>phrases</u> and <u>language</u> <u>devices</u> have been identified to help you.

RICHARD III

<u>Now</u> <u>is</u> the <u>winter</u> <u>of</u> <u>our</u> <u>discontent</u>
<u>Made</u> <u>glorious</u> <u>summer</u> <u>by</u> <u>this</u> <u>sun</u> <u>of</u> <u>York</u>:
And <u>all</u> <u>the</u> <u>clouds</u> <u>that</u> <u>lour'd</u> <u>upon</u> <u>our</u> <u>house</u>
<u>In</u> <u>the</u> <u>deep</u> <u>bosom</u> <u>of</u> <u>the</u> <u>ocean</u> <u>buried</u>
Now are our brows bound with victorious wreaths;
<u>Our</u> <u>bruised</u> <u>arms</u> <u>hung</u> <u>up</u> <u>for</u> <u>monuments</u>;
<u>Our</u> <u>stern</u> <u>alarums</u> <u>chang'd</u> <u>to</u> <u>merry</u> <u>meetings</u>,
<u>Our</u> <u>dreadful</u> <u>marches</u> <u>to</u> <u>delightful</u> <u>measures</u>.
<u>Grim-visag'd</u> <u>war</u> <u>hath</u> <u>smooth'd</u> <u>his</u> <u>wrinkled</u> <u>front</u>;
And now, <u>instead</u> <u>of</u> <u>mounting</u> <u>barbed</u> <u>steeds</u>,
<u>To</u> <u>fright</u> <u>the</u> <u>souls</u> <u>of</u> <u>fearful</u> <u>adversaries</u>,
<u>He</u> <u>capers</u> <u>nimbly</u> <u>in</u> <u>a</u> <u>lady's</u> <u>chamber</u>,
<u>To</u> <u>the</u> <u>lavicious</u> <u>pleasing</u> <u>of</u> <u>a</u> <u>lute</u>,
But I, that am not shap'd for sportive tricks,
Nor made to court an amorous looking-glass;
<u>I</u> <u>that</u> <u>am</u> <u>rudely</u> <u>stamp'd</u> <u>and</u> <u>want</u> <u>loves</u> <u>majesty</u>,

***

I am determined to prove a villain,
And <u>hate</u> <u>the</u> <u>idle</u> <u>pleasures</u> <u>of</u> <u>these</u> <u>days</u>.
<u>Plots</u> <u>have</u> <u>I</u> <u>laid</u>, <u>inductions</u> <u>dangerous</u>,
<u>By</u> <u>drunken</u> <u>prophesies</u>, <u>libels</u> <u>and</u> <u>dreams</u>,
To set my brother Clarence and the king
In deadly hate the one against the other:

Richard III (Act 1, Scene 1, lines 1–16, 30–35)

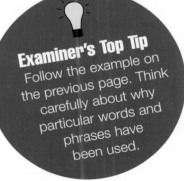

Examiner's Top Tip
Follow the example on the previous page. Think carefully about why particular words and phrases have been used.

SHAKESPEARE TEST

- Always use the bullet points with the question to help plan your answer. The mark scheme is based on these bullet points.
- Remember you must support your opinions with relevant quotations and textual evidence.
- These mock exam questions are very general so that they can be applied to any scene. Try to answer these questions for your specified scenes.

Staging

You are the director of the play. Write detailed instructions for how each of the main characters should be played in these scenes:
Think about:
how they should move
how they should behave
how they should speak
what their relationships should be with other characters.

Literary Criticism

Choose the most appropriate question for your scene from the list below. With all questions you should consider the following:
the behaviour of the characters
use of language
what has happened before the scene and what happens next.

How is the atmosphere created or changed in these scenes?
Think about:
How the characters would behave
What the main characters would be thinking – are they hiding anything?
What has just happened or is about to happen.

Comment on the behaviour of the main character in these scenes.
Think about:
How they behave towards other characters
The language that they use
What is happening in the two scenes.

How are relationships developed in these scenes?
Think about:
The way the characters behave towards each other
The language they use
Have the events of the play affected these characters directly?

Why are these scenes important to the play's development?
Think about:
What happens before and after these scenes
The way the main characters behave in these scenes.

The main characters are under pressure in these scenes. How do they respond to that pressure?
Think about:
What they do
The language they use
How their behaviour may have changed
What happens next.

SPELLING

The best ways to improve your spelling are:
* learn spelling rules
* learn commonly misspelt words
* practise spelling strategies.

TO ACHIEVE LEVEL 5 YOU NEED TO:
* spell <u>basic</u> <u>words</u> and <u>regular</u> <u>polysyllabic</u> <u>words</u> (words with more than one syllable) correctly. In other words, you should be able to spell words that follow spelling rules and fit into patterns with other words.

TO ACHIEVE AT LEVELS 6 AND 7 YOU ALSO NEED TO:
* spell <u>irregular</u> <u>polysyllabic</u> <u>words</u> (words that do not fit patterns and are more commonly misspelt).

SPELLING, PUNCTUATION AND GRAMMAR

Your <u>spelling</u>, <u>punctuation</u> and <u>grammar</u> will only be assessed directly in the <u>final</u> <u>section</u> of <u>Paper One</u> and in <u>Paper</u> <u>Two</u> <u>of</u> <u>the</u> <u>SATS</u>. However, the more accurate your writing is, the more clearly you will be able to express your meaning.

punctuation marks

PUNCTUATION

TO ACHIEVE LEVEL 5 YOU NEED TO:
* use <u>full</u> <u>stops</u>, <u>capital</u> <u>letters</u> and <u>question</u> <u>marks</u> accurately
* use <u>commas</u> within a sentence
* use <u>apostrophes</u> and <u>speech</u> <u>marks</u> correctly.

TO MOVE FROM LEVEL 5 TO LEVELS 6 AND 7 YOU ALSO NEED TO:
* use punctuation to develop a <u>range</u> <u>of</u> <u>complex</u> <u>sentences</u>.

GRAMMAR

TO ACHIEVE LEVEL 5 YOU NEED TO:
* clearly <u>structure</u> your writing <u>using</u> <u>paragraphs</u>
* use a range of <u>simple</u> and <u>complex</u> <u>sentences</u>
* use a <u>wide</u> <u>range</u> <u>of</u> <u>vocabulary</u>.

TO ACHIEVE LEVEL 6 AND 7 YOU ALSO NEED TO:
* show <u>increasing</u> <u>control</u> <u>of a</u> <u>range of</u> <u>sentence</u> <u>types</u>
* use punctuation to <u>clarify</u> <u>meaning</u> and <u>create</u> <u>effects</u>.

SPELLING STRATEGIES

LOOK – SAY – COVER – WRITE – CHECK

<u>Look</u> at the word you want to learn – try to find patterns, learn the shape of the word.

<u>Say</u> the word.

<u>Cover</u> the word with your hand and <u>write</u> it down.

<u>Check</u> your spelling. If you made a mistake go back to the beginning and <u>look</u> carefully at the part of the word you got wrong.

USE A DICTIONARY

Use a dictionary to check the spelling of words you are unsure of. Many dictionaries will also give you information about the roots and origins of words: this is sometimes helpful in learning a new spelling.

<u>Unfortunately, you can't use a dictionary in your exam.</u>

MNEMONICS

Some people find spellings easier to remember if they make up a rhyme to go with it, for example:

<u>R</u>hythm <u>h</u>as <u>y</u>our <u>t</u>wo <u>h</u>ands <u>m</u>oving (<u>rhythm</u>).

<u>B</u>ig <u>e</u>lephants <u>c</u>an't <u>a</u>lways <u>u</u>se <u>s</u>mall <u>e</u>xits (<u>because</u>).

SAY THE WORD AS IT IS SPELT

Words that have silent letters or unstressed syllables in them are often easier to remember if you sound the part of the word that is usually silent. For example:
We<u>dne</u>sday, lis<u>te</u>n, pe<u>op</u>le.

BREAK WORDS INTO PARTS

Polysyllabic words can be broken into smaller chunks to make them easier to remember. It is almost impossible to spell a word completely incorrectly. Work out which part of a word you find difficult and learn it. For example
ex – plan – a – <u>tion</u>

PLURALS

- The following rules will help you with your spelling. However, you need to look out for the exceptions to these rules. Unfortunately, there are quite a lot of them!
- There are some examples for you to try with each rule. Answers on page 95.

–S –ES

Rule: To make a word into a plural add –s
- school – schools   shoe – shoes
  book – books
If a word ends in –ss –sh –ch –x –zz, add –es
- lunch – lunches   glass – glasses   box – boxes

Exceptions: The other rules and conventions on this page show the exceptions to the simple plural rule.

Examiner's Top Tip
Words that end in a hissing, shushing or buzzing sound add –es. When you say –es plurals aloud you can hear an extra syllable.

Quick Questions
add –s or –es:
bench fox church pupil light wish wash

–Y

Rule: If a word ends in a vowel then –y, you add –s. If a word ends in a consonant then –y, you change the –y to –i and add –es.
-        toy – toys key – keys
try – tries factory – factories

Quick Questions
add –s or change the ending: boy fry fly monkey play baby lady

NO-CHANGE PLURALS

Some words don't change at all
- sheep   deer

Examiner's Top Tip
The rules for words ending in –f and –y apply when you are adding any other ending.

–O

Words that end in –o or –oo don't follow set patterns. Try to group words together as you learn them.
- tomato   potato   mango – <u>all edible and all end in –es</u>
- <u>tomatoes   potatoes   mangoes</u>
- toma<u>toes</u>   pota<u>toes</u>   mosqui<u>toes</u> – <u>they all have toes in them</u>
- disco – disco<u>s</u>   tattoo - tatoo<u>s</u>

Quick Questions
radio volcano shampoo go (use a dictionary if you need to)

–F –FF –FE

Any words that end in –ff need an –s to make them plural, for example:
- sheriff – sheriff<u>s</u> cuff – cuff<u>s</u>

Words that end in –<u>f</u> or –<u>fe</u> are more difficult. Some are made plural by adding –<u>s</u>, such as:
- chief – chief<u>s</u>   reef – reef<u>s</u>

Other words change the –<u>f</u> to –<u>v</u> and add –<u>es</u>, such as:
- wife – wi<u>ves</u>   leaf – lea<u>ves</u>   calf – cal<u>ves</u>

Some words that end in –<u>f</u> can be spelled with either an –<u>fs</u> or a –<u>ves</u> plural ending, such as:
- scarf – scar<u>fs</u> or scar<u>ves</u>   hoof – hoofs or hoo<u>ves</u>

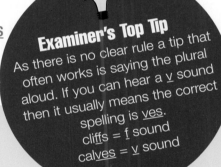

Examiner's Top Tip
As there is no clear rule a tip that often works is saying the plural aloud. If you can hear a <u>v</u> sound then it usually means the correct spelling is <u>ves</u>.
cli<u>ffs</u> = <u>f</u> sound
cal<u>ves</u> = <u>v</u> sound

Quick Questions
– add –s or change the ending:
wolf knife life loaf roof

IRREGULAR PLURALS

Some plural forms don't seem to follow any of these rules and the whole word changes.
- mouse – <u>mice</u>   child – <u>children</u>

You need to <u>learn</u> these words as you meet them.

Examiner's Top Tip
Foreign words follow different rules. Learn them as you need them, e.g. cactus – <u>cacti</u>, fungus – <u>fungi</u>.

Quick Questions
write out the plurals of these words:
man woman goose foot

SUFFIXES

ADDING –ED AND –ING

<u>Rule</u>: If the word ends in a single consonant and the syllable is stressed, you double the consonant when you add the ending. If the syllable is not stressed, you just add the ending.

- stop – sto<u>pp</u>ed – sto<u>pp</u>ing
- fit – fi<u>tt</u>ed – fi<u>tt</u>ing
- focus – focu<u>s</u>ed – focu<u>s</u>ing

If the word ends in -e you only add the -<u>d</u> of -<u>ed</u>. You omit the -<u>e</u> if you are adding -<u>ing</u>.

- continue – continue<u>d</u>
- mak<u>e</u> – making

ADDING –FUL

<u>Rule</u>: Remember full becomes -<u>ful</u>. You do not change the original word unless it ends in y (see y ending rule).

- **fit – fit<u>ful</u>**
- **hope – hope<u>ful</u>**

ADDING –LY

<u>Rule</u>: The original word does not change when you add -<u>ly</u>.

- real – real<u>ly</u>
- proper – proper<u>ly</u>
- careful – carefu<u>lly</u>

watch out for exceptions to the rule e.g. words that end in -ie: remove the -e and add -y

Examiner's Top Tip
Learning prefix and suffix rules will help to spell polysyllabic words.

WORDS ENDING IN –Y OR –F

<u>Rule</u>: The rule for adding suffixes to words ending in –y or –f are the same as the pluralising rules.

- **fry – fr<u>ied</u>**
- **beauty – beauti<u>ful</u>**
- **happy – happ<u>ily</u>**
- **play – pla<u>yed</u>**
- **shelf – shel<u>ving</u>**

PREFIXES AND SUFFIXES

- A <u>prefix</u> is two or three letters added to the beginning of a word to change or qualify the meaning, for example, <u>dis-</u> <u>mis-</u> <u>pre-</u> <u>un-</u>.
- A <u>suffix</u> is two or three letters added to the end of a word to make a derivative of the original word, for example, <u>-ed</u> <u>-ful</u> <u>-ing</u> <u>-ly</u> <u>-ment</u>. Sometimes adding a suffix <u>changes</u> the spelling of the original word.

PREFIXES

<u>Rule</u>: When you add a prefix you <u>do</u> <u>not</u> change the spelling of the original word.

- satisfied – <u>dis</u>satisfied
- spelling – <u>mis</u>spelling
- necessary – <u>un</u>necessary

Quick Questions

How many words can you make from these <u>prefixes</u> and <u>suffixes</u>?

PREFIX	ROOT	SUFFIX
mis	appoint	ment
pre	fortunate	ful
dis	view	ly
un	event	ed
	understand	ing

Examiner's Top Tip
Remember: prefixes never change the root word.

HOMOPHONES

The best way to ensure that you get them right is to learn them. Some ideas that might help you to learn them are:
- look for patterns
- make groups of words that have similar spellings or meanings
- draw pictures or cartoons
- make up rhymes.

Are:	**present form of the verb to be, e.g. <u>Where are you going</u>? <u>We are all the same age</u>.**
Our:	**belonging to us**
Hear:	**to perceive sound,** **e.g. <u>Can you hear me</u>?** 
Here:	**referring to place,** **e.g. <u>Come over here</u>.**
Their:	**belonging to them**
There:	**referring to place,** **Indicates the fact or existence of something e.g. <u>There is a horse in the field</u>.** 
They're:	**short form of <u>they are</u>**
Threw:	**past tense of throw,** **e.g. <u>He threw the ball</u>.** 
Through:	**<u>He went through the door</u>. <u>I read the letter through, from beginning to end</u>.**
To:	**introduces a noun or a verb, e.g. <u>Are you going to</u>** *noun* → **<u>school</u>? <u>I was going to</u>** *verb* → **<u>walk today</u>.** 
Too:	**1. also/as well, e.g. <u>Can we come too</u>?** **2. excessive, e.g. <u>It was too hot</u>. <u>That is too expensive</u>.**
Two:	**the number 2**

HOMOPHONES/ BASIC WORDS

- There are many words in the English language that sound the same but are spelt differently and have different meanings. They are known as <u>homophones</u>.
- Many of these words are basic words that are commonly used in everyday writing.

<u>Saw</u>:	1. past tense of see, e.g. <u>I</u> <u>saw</u> <u>you</u> <u>taking</u> <u>it</u>.
	2. tool to cut wood, e.g. <u>Pass</u> <u>me</u> <u>the</u> <u>saw</u>.
<u>Soar</u>:	to fly or rise high, e.g. <u>The</u> <u>eagle</u> <u>soared</u> <u>high</u> <u>in</u> <u>the</u> <u>sky</u>.
<u>Sore</u>:	painful, e.g. <u>My</u> <u>leg</u> <u>was</u> <u>sore</u>.
<u>Wear</u>:	of clothes, etc., e.g. <u>I</u> <u>wear</u> <u>school</u> <u>uniform</u>.
<u>Were</u>:	past tense of are, e.g. <u>We</u> <u>are</u> <u>going</u> <u>to</u> <u>school</u>./<u>We</u> <u>were</u> <u>going</u> <u>to</u> <u>school</u>.
<u>We're</u>:	short form of <u>we</u> <u>are</u>
<u>Where</u>:	referring to place, e.g. <u>Where</u> <u>is</u> <u>it</u>?
<u>Who's</u>:	short form of <u>who</u> <u>is</u>
<u>Whose</u>:	belonging to someone

Use this space to record other homophones with which you have trouble. Use some of the strategies to learn and remember them.

....
....
....
....
....

Examiner's Top Tip
The word 'there' has many different uses. '<u>Their</u>' and '<u>they're</u>' have only one use each. Learn the use of <u>their</u> and <u>they're</u> first; <u>there</u> is used on all other occasions.

WORDS THAT ARE OFTEN MISSPELLED

WORD	RULE/HINT
A**cc**ept**able**	use <u>able</u> if the rest of the word will stand alone – <u>accept</u>
A**cc**o**mm**odation	
Ach**ie**ve	<u>i</u> before <u>e</u> except after <u>c</u>
Anal**y**se	
A**ss**e**ss**	
Bel**ie**ve	
Co**mm**unicate	
Conv**e**ni**e**nt	
Defin**ite**	
Desp**e**rate	
Di**s**a**pp**ear	root words never change when you add a prefix
Di**s**a**pp**oint	root words never change when you add a prefix
Ne**c**e**ss**ary	<u>n</u>ever <u>e</u>at <u>c</u>ake <u>e</u>at <u>s</u>alad <u>s</u>andwiches and <u>r</u>emain <u>y</u>oung
	one <u>c</u>ollar and two <u>s</u>ocks
Perm**a**n**e**nt	
Pers**ua**de	
<u>Phy</u>sical	
Rec**ei**ve	<u>i</u> before <u>e</u> except after <u>c</u>
Reco**mm**end	
Respons**ible**	use <u>ible</u> if the rest of the word <u>will</u> <u>not</u> stand alone – <u>respons</u>
Sep**ara**te	there's <u>a</u> <u>rat</u> in sep<u>ara</u>te
Station**a**ry	not moving
Station**e**ry	paper, etc.
Su**cc**e**ss**	
Su**r**prise	
We**i**rd	a weird exception to the rule!

Don't forget to ...

<u>Look</u>   <u>say</u>   <u>cover</u>   <u>write</u>   <u>check</u>

to learn these words!

COMMONLY MISSPELT WORDS

- The words on the lefthand page are often spelt wrongly. It is a good idea to learn them as they sometimes fail to fit into normal spelling rules.
- The parts of the words that cause confusion or difficulty have been underlined.

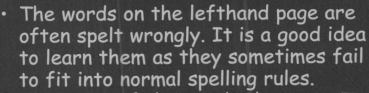

USE THIS PAGE TO RECORD SPELLINGS WITH WHICH YOU HAVE DIFFICULTY.

CAPITAL LETTERS AND FULL STOPS

Capital letters and full stops show where a sentence begins and ends:
- the cat was sick in the morning we decided to take it to the vet
- The cat was sick. In the morning we decided to take it to the vet.

CAPITAL LETTERS ARE ALSO USED FOR:
- the word 'I'
- acronyms: BBC, RAC
- names of people, places and products: Jane, Brazil, Weetabix.

PUNCTUATION MARKS

When we talk, we use different tones of voice and we pause after certain words to make our meaning clear. When we write, we use punctuation to make our meaning clear.

COMMAS

Commas help us to understand the meaning within a sentence. They are used to:

- **separate items in a list**
You will need a pen, a pencil, a ruler and a rubber.

- **separate additional information from the rest of the sentence**
John, who was very angry, shouted at the children.

- **separate subordinate clauses from main clauses**
When the rope snapped, the climber fell and broke her leg.

subordinate

main

- **after the following words:**
however, therefore, of course, nevertheless.

88

COLONS AND SEMICOLONS

- Colons are advanced punctuation marks. They point ahead to something which follows. This could be a quotation in an essay or the beginning of a list.
- The semicolon is another advanced mark of punctuation. They are used to join two sentences which are very closely linked; this may be where a full stop seems too strong and a comma too weak.
- Semicolons are also used to separate items in a list when they are phrases rather than single words:

Before you go out you should: tidy your bedroom; wash the dishes; feed the cat and hang the washing out.

SPEECH PUNCTUATION

Speech marks are essential in your writing to show clearly that someone has spoken. There is a lot more to punctuating speech than just speech marks. Here are some basic rules to follow:

- Speech marks "…" or '…' are placed around the words a person actually speaks.
- The first word inside the speech marks always begins with a capital letter.
- The words inside speech marks always end with a mark of punctuation (full stop, comma, question mark or exclamation mark).
- If the sentence is continued after the speech marks (with he said, etc.), then you don't end the speech with a full stop, and the first word outside the speech marks must begin with a small letter.
- If the sentence begins with he said a comma must follow this before you open the speech marks.
- When a new speaker begins, you must begin a new paragraph.

Example
'Tidy your bedroom before you go out,'
said my mother.
The man turned and whispered,
'Never ask me that again.'

Quick Questions

Add the correct punctuation to these sentences:
1. shut up shouted james you don't know what you're talking about
2. i want to go home now mum whispered the bored child
3. have you seen my sister asked simon no i haven't seen her since yesterday said Julie
4. i saw james the boy who broke his leg on the bbc news last night
5. when the bell rang the teacher dismissed the class
6. my sister who's a nurse helped to bandage my leg

Answers on page 95.

APOSTROPHES AND PARAGRAPHS

There are <u>two</u> ways to use <u>apostrophes</u>:
• to indicate omission   • to indicate possession.
There are <u>three</u> ways to organise <u>paragraphs</u>:
• by time   • by topic   • by talk.

Examiner's Top Tip
Proper planning will al
you to structure yo
writing more effectiv

POSSESSION

Apostrophes are used to show that something belongs to someone or something.
• John<u>'</u>s bag – the bag belonging to John

When something belongs to a single person or thing, add apostrophe and s.
• the cat<u>'</u>s whiskers; Sally<u>'</u>s coat; the boy<u>'</u>s homework

If the word already ends in s, then just add an apostrophe after the s.
• James<u>'</u> book

When something belongs to more than one person or thing add an apostrophe after the s.
• the cats<u>'</u> whiskers; the girls<u>'</u> bags; ladies<u>'</u> coats

If the plural form of a word does not end in s, then add an apostrophe and s.
• the children<u>'</u>s homework; the men<u>'</u>s hats

It is not just objects that belong to people: emotions, people and actions also belong.
• Susan<u>'</u>s anger; Amanda<u>'</u>s fear; John<u>'</u>s father; the poet<u>'</u>s writing
'Belonging to it' does not follow the above rules.
<u>its</u> = <u>belonging</u> to it
<u>it's</u> = <u>it is</u>

OMISSION

<u>Apostrophes</u> are used to show that a letter, or letters, have been missed out when writing a short form of a word. For example: <u>cannot</u> becomes <u>can't</u>.

If you remember <u>why</u> apostrophes are used then you should always get them in the right place.

People often think that the apostrophe goes between the two words that are being joined: <u>this</u> <u>is</u> <u>wrong</u>.

- <u>does</u> <u>+</u> <u>not</u> = <u>does'nt</u> ✗
- <u>does</u> <u>+</u> <u>not</u> = <u>doesnt</u> = <u>doesn't</u> ✔
- <u>it</u> <u>+</u> <u>is</u> = <u>it's</u> ✔

PARAGRAPHS

- A paragraph is a group of sentences linked to the same topic.
- Paragraphs help you to organise your work.
- In handwriting, indicate paragraphs by starting a new line and indenting about one centimetre from the margin.

Look at this extract from *A Kestrel for a Knave*. Notice how the paragraphs are organised.

topic / time
Billy tried another rush. Sugden repelled it, so he tried the other end again. Every time he tried to escape the three boys bounced him back, stinging him with their snapping towels as he retreated ....

topic
When Billy stopped yelling the other boys stopped laughing, and when time passed and no more was heard from him, their conversations began to peter out, and attention gradually focused on the showers ....

talk
The boy guards began to look uneasy, and they looked across to their captain.
'Can we let him out now, Sir?'
'No!'

Quick Questions

Write out the short forms of these words using apostrophes:

do not _____
they will _____
have not _____
I am _____
would not _____

Add the possessive apostrophes: _____
the mans strength _____
the girls bags (singular) _____
the girls bags (plural) _____
yesterdays meeting _____
Lauras ambition _____

Answers on page 95.

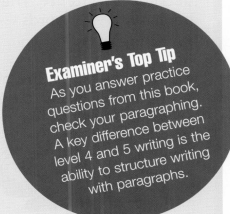

Examiner's Top Tip
As you answer practice questions from this book, check your paragraphing. A key difference between level 4 and 5 writing is the ability to structure writing with paragraphs.

SENTENCES

There are three types of sentence:
1.   simple
2.   compound
3.   complex.
A sentence usually contains a <u>subject</u> and a <u>verb</u>.

<u>My</u> <u>sister</u> <u>runs</u> <u>in</u> <u>the</u> <u>park.</u>
subject   verb   phrase   (in this case information
                                              about where it happens)

SIMPLE SENTENCES
These give you one main piece of information:
• I ran home. I was late. My mum was angry.
If you want to achieve <u>level 5</u> and above you need to use a range of sentences – simple, compound and complex.

COMPOUND SENTENCES
These are made up from simple sentences joined together by <u>conjunctions</u> – <u>and</u>, <u>but</u> and <u>or</u>.
• I ran home. I was late and my mum was angry but she didn't tell me off.

COMPLEX SENTENCES
These are made up of two or more clauses, one of which must be a subordinate clause. A <u>clause</u> has a <u>subject</u> and contains a <u>verb</u>.

RELATIVE CLAUSES
This is a kind of subordinate clause, which allows you to add more detail to a sentence. They begin with <u>wh</u>- words – <u>who</u> or <u>which</u>.

• My shoes, <u>which</u> are old and smelly, need to be thrown away.

SUBORDINATE CLAUSES
<u>Subordinate</u> <u>clauses</u> give background information about when something happened or how people feel. They help you to create two-part sentences. These clauses always begin with words like <u>although</u>, <u>however</u>, <u>because</u>, <u>before</u>. Subordinate clauses can be used in the first or second half of a sentence.

• <u>Although</u> <u>her</u> <u>feet</u> <u>hurt</u>, <u>Jane</u> <u>carried</u> <u>on</u> <u>running</u>.
subordinate   main
• <u>The</u> <u>children</u> <u>played</u> <u>outside</u>, <u>despite</u> <u>the</u> <u>fact</u> <u>that</u> <u>it</u> <u>was</u> <u>raining</u>.
main   subordinate

GRAMMAR

Grammar is the way we organise words to make sense.
'This is my dog' is grammatical and it makes sense.
'My this is dog' is ungrammatical; it makes no sense at all.

PARTS OF SPEECH

NOUNS
Common: an object you can see or touch, e.g. pen, table, car.
Abstract: thoughts, ideas, qualities or emotions, e.g. peace, anger, truth.
Collective: one word indicating a collection of people or objects,
e.g. group, herd, queue.
Proper: an individual name; a place, a person or an object,
e.g. Birmingham, Jane, Tower of London.

PRONOUNS
A pronoun takes the place of a noun that has already
been mentioned: he, she, it, me, you. Use of pronouns
helps to reduce repetition in your writing. John picked
up the ball and threw the ball to John's friend. John
picked up the ball and threw it to his friend.

ADJECTIVES
An adjective is a describing word. It tells us what a
noun is like: old book, sensible child, smelly socks.
The use of adjectives in your writing will make
it more interesting.

VERBS
A verb makes a noun or pronoun work. There are two
types of verb.
Main: as a general rule you can put the word 'to' in
front of a main verb, e.g. to walk, to dance, to eat.
Auxiliary: an auxiliary verb helps the
main verb, e.g. you should walk,
he could dance, I might eat.

ADVERBS
An adverb is a describing word. It tells us how
a verb is done, e.g. he walked quickly, he danced
stylishly, I ate greedily.

Reading Fiction

1. Exclamation and question marks **(1 mark)** indicate that they are shouting and there is a lot of disagreement **(1 mark)**

2. Billy is compared to a Jewish child in a concentration camp hurrying towards his death in the shower; because he is thin and dirty he looks like a victim – then what happens to him in the showers is like torture; emphasizes the abuse of power; if Billy is like a concentration camp victim then Mr Sugden must be compared to a Nazi. **(3 marks)**

3. Marks will be awarded as follows: **1–2 marks (level 3)** for a simple, generalised comment which relates to just one bullet point or repeats the prompts **3 marks (level 4)** supports general comment about one bullet point with detail from the text **4 marks (level 5)** supports general comment with detail from the text and addresses all bullet points **5 marks (level 6)** addresses all of the bullet points, making specific comments supported by explanation and a range of detail from the text. **6 marks (level 7)** does all of the above, focusing on aspects of language and structure and giving a personal response.

Reading Poetry

1. Sample answers include: *hard as a knot* – makes you think of the texture of rope, the berries would be unpleasant and difficult to eat; *palms sticky as Bluebeard's* – the children imagine that the juice is like blood on their hands, like the famous pirate Bluebeard, which shows that collecting the blackberries is an exciting adventure **(2 marks for 1 similes and explanation)**

2. *hoarded* and *cache*, the image is of pirates storing their treasure, the berries are precious to the boy, collecting the berries is an exciting adventure, the boys might play a game like "pirates" **(3 marks for 2 words and explanation)**

3. Long sentences and use of enjambment keep the poem moving forward; mirrors the children running through the fields, the urgency of filling up all the containers with berries **(2 marks)** words like milk-cans, pea-tins, are tricky to say one after the other, you have to skip over them lightly, again this reflects the movement of the children **(2 marks)**

Reading Non-Fiction

1. 'Like a beetle walking into a dawn patrol of ants' **(1 mark)** creates the feeling of ambush and surprise; emphasises the feeling of being surrounded and swarmed over; evokes the surroundings of the country. **(2 marks)**

2. effective because it builds up feelings of helplessness and captivity; describes a series of helplessness and captivity; describes a series of basic danger-avoiding techniques she cannot do – frustration and fear; makes us aware of the barriers she faced. **(2 marks)**

3. see answer to Q3 in **Reading Fiction**

Reading Media Tests

1. Sample answers include: Fact – "operates 24 hours a day" information about the service, makes it seem reliable. Opinion – "we'll always be there for you" reassuring, makes the service providers seem like friends. **(4 marks)**

2. Personal pronouns: you and we; makes the leaflet

personalised, a direct invitation to the reader to find out more. This would particularly appeal to older people who feel lonely or live away from their family. **(2 marks)**

3. see answer to Q3 in **Reading Fiction**

Writing Test Paper 1

This mark scheme will be used to assess your writing.

A: Sentence structure and punctuation

Ideas and sentences are mostly linked using conjunctions such as 'and', 'but' and 'when'. Sentences are mainly compound. Full stops, capital letters, question marks and exclamation marks are used mostly accurately. **(1 mark)** Sentences are varied; relative clauses are used. Subordinating conjunctions, develop reasons and emphasis. Commas are used within sentences, mainly with accuracy. **(2 marks)** Compound and complex sentences are used. Phrases and clauses build up detail and give information. A variety of punctuation is used with accuracy. Different types of sentence including exclamations, commands and questions add interest and variety. **(3 marks)** Shades of meaning are expressed through the use of a range of grammatical structures. A range of punctuation is used with accuracy; sometimes used to create deliberate effects. **(4 marks)** Sentence structure is varied as appropriate. Simple sentences are used effectively and contrasts achieve particular effects. Punctuation is used with accuracy to clarify meaning and vary pace. **(5 marks)**

Paragraph organisation/textual cohesion

Ideas are linked mainly through topic. Points listed in no particular order of importance. **(1 mark)** Paragraphs generally open with the main idea and contain examples or illustrations. **(2 marks)** Paragraphs are logically sequenced. There is a sense of introduction and conclusion. Paragraphs of different lengths are used to emphasise ideas or to create feelings of tension or excitement. **(3 marks)** Detailed content is organised well within and between paragraphs. Some connectives are used to show logical relationships. The introduction and conclusion to persuasion and argument contribute to the persuasiveness of the text. Structure of narrative writing is controlled through paragraph length and organization. **(4 marks)** Paragraphs are varied in length to help control ideas. Cohesion of the text is reinforced by the use of a range of linking devices. Paragraph structure is varied to create impact and develop ideas. **(5 marks)**

Composition and effect

The given form of the writing shows some awareness of the reader. There is some relevant content but possibly uneven coverage. **(1–3 marks)** Writing is generally lively and attempts to interest the reader. A sense of purpose is shown in the content of persuasive writing. In narrative writing the plot structure is clear and is balanced with description. **(4–6 marks)** Writing is detailed and gives clear reasons for opinions. It engages the reader's interest. A range of imaginative vocabulary is used to describe people and objects. **(7–9 marks)** A range of persuasive devices is used. Imagery is used in description and alternative narrative structures are explored. **(10–12 marks)** The tone and content of writing is appropriate and well judged. Narrative writing shows control and development of characters and settings. **(13–15 marks)**

Spelling

Simple words are usually accurate. **(1 mark)** Simple and polysyllable words are generally accurate. **(2 marks)** Words with complex but regular patterns are generally accurate. **(3 marks)** Most spelling, including irregular words, is accurate. **(4 marks)** Virtually all spelling, including complex irregular words, is correct. **(5 marks)**

Writing Test Paper 2

This mark scheme will be used to assess your writing.

Vocabulary

A linked range of nouns and adjectives are used with little variation for effect. **(1 mark)** Vocabulary chosen to interest the reader and create some effects. Range of nouns, verbs, adjectives and adverbs are used. **(2 marks)** Vocabulary is creative. Adjectives used to compare and contrast subject nouns. **(3 marks)** Range of inventive and creative vocabulary is used to engage the reader's interest. **(4 marks)**

Sentence structure/punctuation and paragraph organization

Sentences are mainly simple or compound. Parts of sentences and ideas mostly are linked by conjunctions. Full stops and capital letters are used with accuracy. **(1–2 marks)** Sentences are varied through the use of relative clauses. Pronouns are generally used consistently as are tenses. Paragraphs are used appropriately with some sequencing and ordering of detail. **(3–4 marks)** Compound and complex sentences are used, with phrases and clauses being used to build up relevant detail. Punctuation is used correctly. Paragraphs are used appropriately with sequencing of detail. **(5–6 marks)** A range of grammatical structures is used to vary the focus of sentences. Range of punctuation used correctly. Paragraphs are varied in structure and length in order to reflect the content of the writing. **(7–8 marks)**

Composition and effect

Writing shows some awareness of the reader. Although there is relevant content, there is uneven coverage of the prompts given in the question. **(1–2 marks)** Writing makes attempts to engage the reader's interest. Some stylistic devices are used to reinforce the meaning of the piece. The topic is covered adequately, but writing is unimaginative. **(3–4 marks)** The writing engages the reader's interest. There is a secure sense of purpose. The setting is developed, and various devices are used to communicate meaning. A coherent viewpoint is presented. **(5–6 marks)** The writing engages the reader's interest. Full range of appropriate details and ideas included. Viewpoint of the writer consistently maintained. Good balance between description, information and explanation. **(7–8 marks)**

Shakespeare Test

Use the following level descriptors as a guide:

Level 3 A simple retelling of the scenes. No reference to the text.

Level 4 A few simple comments about the characters. Answer focuses on retelling the scenes. Some reference to the text but no supporting explanation.

Level 5 Answer contains a straightforward commentary on the scenes. Displays a good level of understanding of characters and their motivation. Comments are supported by reference to the text.

Level 6 A focused answer with a degree of exploration of the text. Detailed commentary displays understanding of characters, motivation and relationships. Some awareness of language used and how this contributes to character and atmosphere. References to the text are appropriate and relevant.

Level 7 Answer shows knowledge of the text and the characters and focuses on the requirements of the question. A good understanding of how language contributes to the exploration of characters, motivation, relationships and themes. Answer shows insight and gives some personal response. Comments are justified by carefully selected reference to the text.

Spelling – plurals

Benches, foxes, churches, pupils, lights, wishes, washes, boys, fried, flies, monkeys, plays, babies, ladies, wolves, knives, lives, loaves, roofs, men, women, geese, feet, radios, volcanoes, shampoos, goes

Spelling – prefixes and suffixes

Misunderstand, misunderstanding, understanding, understandingly, preview, previewed, previewing, viewed, viewing, disappoint, disappointment, disappointed, disappointing, appointment, appointed, appointing, uneventful, uneventfully, eventful, eventfully, unfortunate, unfortunately, fortunately

Punctuation

"Shut up!" shouted James. "You don't know what you're talking about."
"I want to go home now mum," whispered the bored child.
"Have you seen my sister?" asked Simon.
"No I haven't seen her since yesterday," said Julie.
I saw James, the boy who broke his leg, on the BBC news last night.
When the bell rang, the teacher dismissed the class.
My sister, who's a nurse, helped to bandage my leg.

Apostrophes

Don't, they'll, haven't, I'm, wouldn't, the man's strength, the girl's bags, (singular), the girls' bags (plural), yesterday's meeting, Laura's ambition